the **egg** book

the **egg** book

hamlyn

First published in Great Britain in 2003 by
Hamlyn, a division of Octopus Publishing Group Ltd
2–4 Heron Quays, London E14 4JP

ISBN 0 600 60839 5

A CIP catalogue record for this book is available from the British Library

Printed and bound in China

10 9 8 7 6 5 4 3 2 1

NOTES

1 The Department of Health advises that eggs should not be consumed raw. It is prudent for more vulnerable people such as pregnant and nursing mothers, invalids, the elderly, babies and young children to avoid uncooked or lightly cooked dishes made with eggs.

2 Meat and poultry should be cooked thoroughly. To test if poultry is cooked, pierce the flesh through the thickest part with a skewer or fork – the juices should run clear, never pink or red.

3 This book includes dishes made with nuts and nut derivatives. It is advisable for those with known allergic reactions to nuts and nut derivatives and those who may be potentially vulnerable to these allergies, such as pregnant and nursing mothers, invalids, the elderly, babies and children, to avoid dishes made with nuts and nut oils. It is also prudent to check the labels of pre-prepared ingredients for the possible inclusion of nut derivatives.

contents

egg facts

The egg is probably the most universal form of food; eggs are found all over the world, eaten at all times of day – breakfast, lunch, tea, dinner and supper, as well as at picnics and in packed meals – and on every sort of social gathering from the grandest to the most humble.

Edible eggs

Unless otherwise qualified, an egg always means a hen's egg. However, they are not the only form of edible eggs. Other eggs found on the menu range in size from tiny quails' eggs to ostrich eggs, which are large enough to make an omelette for 8–10 people. Guinea fowl, gull, bantam and duck eggs can also be found commercially with varying degrees of frequency and are worth trying.

Nutrition

Eggs are a valuable source of protein and rich in calcium, iron, zinc, the B group vitamins and vitamins A, D, E and K. They are a concentrated source of nutrients and help promote good bones and joints. They also boost the immune system. However, eggs should not be consumed raw and it is advisable for more vulnerable people such as pregnant and nursing mothers, invalids, the elderly, babies and young children to avoid uncooked or lightly cooked egg dishes. Despite the widely held belief, there is no difference in flavour or nutritional quality between brown and white eggs.

Choosing eggs

Eggs are sold by size, graded into very large, large, medium and small. As a general rule, choose large eggs for recipes. Very large and large are a good choice for boiling, frying, poaching, scrambling and omelettes, while smaller eggs are useful for binding ingredients or for glazing.

Storing eggs

Cool storage is essential to keep eggs fresh, but remember to remove them from the refrigerator 20–30 minutes before use. Store eggs with the pointed end downwards – this means the yolk will stay in the centre of the egg – and keep them away from strong-smelling foods as the porous shell will absorb smells and flavours. Try not to keep eggs for more than two weeks; instead, buy them in smaller quantities to use them up more quickly.

Leftover whites and yolks can be stored in small covered containers in the refrigerator. Yolks, if whole, should be covered with a little water to keep them moist: they should be used within about 24 hours.

Testing for freshness

Very fresh eggs are best for poaching and whisking, and are also easier to separate. Because egg shells are porous, allowing moisture to evaporate from the white and air to enter, this forms a pocket between the shell and the lining membrane. The older an egg is, the larger the air pocket at the rounded end of the shell. This acts as a float, so a quick test can be used to indicate the freshness of an egg.

Dissolve 1 tablespoon salt in 600 ml/ 1 pint water and lower the egg into it. A very fresh egg will sink and lie on its side. If it lies at a slight angle it is about a week old and if it tilts straight upwards or floats it is stale.

Another test is to break the egg on to a plate. If the egg is fresh, the yolk will stand clearly above the white, as a plump dome, and the white will have two distinct layers: around the yolk it will be thick and gelatinous, with a distinctly thinner outer layer. A stale

egg has a flatter yolk, with less distinction between the two layers of egg white.

Separating eggs

Many recipes require only the white of an egg, or the yolk. Whisked egg whites are used in recipes such as soufflés and meringues (see pages 14–15) as, when cooked, they expand and increase the volume of whatever they are mixed with. The use of egg whites in sorbets has a stablizing effect, minimizing the formation of ice crystals.

Egg yolks can be used as emulsifiers, holding oil or butter in suspension, keeping the two from separating; the classic example of this is mayonnaise (see page 15). Egg yolks also act as a binding agent in stuffings, fish cakes and burgers, holding the surrounding ingredients together.

To separate an egg, tap it against the rim of a bowl to crack it around the middle. Holding the egg over the bowl, carefully open the shell with your thumbs, holding the two halves together to let some of the white run out. Gently tip the yolk from one half of the shell to the other, letting the white run into the bowl and taking care not to break the yolk.

If you are separating more than 1 egg, use a second bowl and tip the whites into the main bowl when separated. If a yolk then breaks, it won't spoil the whole batch of whites. It is important to separate eggs cleanly as even a trace of yolk can prevent the egg white becoming stiff when it is whisked.

Whisking egg whites

A large balloon whisk is the best tool to use, since it incorporates as much air as possible into the whites. However, an electric hand mixer will also give good results. Use a large, wide bowl to allow plenty of air to be whisked in.

Before you start, make absolutely sure that the bowl and whisk are completely clean and grease-free, since any trace of grease will give the whisked whites a poor volume, and you may find they will not whisk stiffly at all.

Begin whisking slowly until the egg whites are broken up and bubbles appear. Then continue to whisk hard and fast until the egg whites begin to hold their shape. Try lifting the whisk from the mixture – at first the whites will hold soft peaks, bending over slightly. If you continue to whisk, the foam will become stiffer and as you lift the whisk the peaks will form stiff points which stay firm and upright.

Depending on the recipe, whisk the whites to soft or stiff peaks, but take care not to overwhisk. Overwhisked whites become dry and powdery, and it is difficult to fold them into a mixture. Use the whisked whites straight away as if they are left to stand, the foam will begin to collapse and the whites cannot be re-whisked.

Folding in egg whites

It is important that the mixture into which you are folding whisked egg whites is neither too hot nor too cold, since either can cause much of the volume to be lost. First lighten the mixture by stirring in 1–2 tablespoons of the whisked whites – this makes it easier to fold in the rest without knocking out too much air. Use a large metal spoon to fold in the whites, with a cutting and folding action, until the mixture is evenly mixed, with no white clumps of foam remaining.

how to cook eggs

Boiled eggs

There are two main methods of boiling eggs (see below). Eggs may crack if plunged straight into boiling water, especially if they are cold. To avoid this, carefully prick the rounded end with a pin before placing them in the saucepan. If the shell does crack, sprinkle a little salt on the crack to help the white set.

Method 1: Cold Water

Put the eggs into a saucepan and pour in enough cold water to cover them completely. Place the pan over a high heat. As soon as the water reaches boiling point, reduce the heat so the water simmers and time the cooking.

COOKING TIMES FOR EGGS (LARGE):

Soft-boiled eggs	3–4 minutes
Firm white, runny yolk	4 minutes
Hard-boiled eggs	10 minutes

Method 2: Hot Water

Lower the eggs into a pan of simmering water to cover them completely. Bring the water back to simmering point and time the cooking.

COOKING TIMES FOR EGGS (LARGE):

Soft-boiled eggs	3–4 minutes
Firm white, runny yolk	7 minutes
Hard-boiled eggs	12 minutes

To prevent hard-boiled eggs overcooking and to avoid the formation of a black ring around the yolk, drain them as soon as they are cooked. Tap the eggs on a hard surface to crack the shell, then leave the eggs in cold water to cool.

Poached eggs

A perfect poached egg is lightly set and compact in shape. You will need very fresh eggs to achieve this.

Pour about 4 cm/½ inch water into a saucepan or frying pan and add 1 tablespoon vinegar. This helps the whites cling to the yolk and makes for a neat shape. Put the pan over a low heat and bring the water just to simmering point – too many bubbles will cause the egg white to break up before it sets.

Break the egg into a cup or small dish and slide it into the water. If necessary, gently stir the water around the egg to draw the white into shape. Leave to poach over a very low heat for 3–5 minutes, until the white is just set, but the yolk is still soft.

Fried eggs

Heat about 2 teaspoons of oil or melted bacon fat in a heavy or nonstick frying pan until really hot.

Break an egg into a cup and quickly tip it into the pan – the white should begin to set immediately. Reduce the heat to medium and spoon the fat over the egg to cook the top surface. Cook for about 1 minute or until the white is set. Use a fish slice to lift the egg from the pan and drain on kitchen paper.

Scrambled eggs

Beat the eggs with a fork, adding salt and pepper to taste. Add 1 tablespoon milk for every 2 eggs if you like a creamy mixture. Melt 15 g/½ oz butter in a heavy or nonstick saucepan and add the eggs, then stir gently with a wooden spoon over a low heat until they are beginning to set. Remove from the heat and serve immediately.

Grated cheese, fresh herbs, strips of smoked salmon or diced cooked bacon make delicious additions to scrambled egg. Simply stir through the egg mixture just before serving.

Baked eggs

To bake eggs *en cocotte*, grease several ramekin dishes with butter, then place them in a roasting tin with 2.5cm/ 1 inch warm water. Break 1 egg into each dish, sprinkle it with salt and pepper and dot the surface with a little butter or one or two tablespoons of cream.

Cook the eggs in a preheated oven, 180°C (350°F), Gas Mark 4, for 8–10 minutes until the eggs are just set. Remove from the pan of water straight away or they will continue cooking. Serve immediately.

Add extra flavour by placing some flaked fish, fried onion or cooked bacon in the bottom of each ramekin before breaking the eggs on top.

Another method of baking eggs is to bake them in small, shallow dishes. Grease each dish with butter, then break an egg into it, and season with salt and pepper and ground nutmeg. Bake in a preheated oven, 180°C (350°F), Gas Mark 4, for 12–15 minutes, according to taste.

Toppings such as grated Parmesan or Cheddar cheese, chopped spring onions or fresh chives can be sprinkled on top before you put the dishes in the oven. Alternatively, line each dish with cooked ham or grated cheese, then break the eggs on top.

basic recipes

omelette

2 eggs
1 tablespoon cold water
15 g/½ oz butter
salt and pepper

1 Break the eggs into a bowl and whisk lightly with a balloon whisk. Whisk in the water and season well with salt and pepper. Do not over beat as this will ruin the texture of the finished omelette.

2 Place the pan over a gentle heat and, when it is hot, add the butter. Tip the pan so that the entire inner surface is coated with butter. When the butter is foaming, but not browned, tip in the eggs.

3 Leave for a few seconds then, using a spatula, draw the mixture away from the edge of the pan into the centre, allowing the eggs to run to the sides. Repeat the process twice more, by which time the eggs should have set. Cook for a further 30 seconds until the underside is golden and top still slightly runny and creamy. Tilt the pan and, with the spatula, carefully turn the omelette on to a plate, folding it in half in the process.

SERVES: 1
PREPARATION TIME: 2 minutes
COOKING TIME: 2 minutes

Variations
Various flavourings and fillings may be added to the basic folded omelette mixture before cooking, such as chopped mixed chives, parsley and tarragon; chopped smoked salmon mixed with a little soured cream; chopped cooked mushrooms and grated Cheddar cheese. The Spanish omelette (see page 50), also known as a tortilla, and Italian frittata (see pages 51–53) are much more substantial. They are cooked for a longer time and served hot, warm or cold.

coating **batter**

60 g/2½ oz self-raising flour
60 g/2½ oz cornflour
pinch of salt
1 tablespoon sunflower oil
150 ml/¼ pint milk or half milk and
half water
1 egg white

1 Sift the flour, cornflour and salt into a large bowl and make a well in the centre. Add the oil and milk or milk and water, then beat until smooth and bubbly. Whisk the egg white in a clean bowl until it holds soft peaks, then fold it quickly into the batter. Use the batter to coat fish fillets, apple rings or vegetable chunks.

MAKES: 250 ml/8 fl oz
PREPARATION TIME: 10 minutes

Variation
For a really crisp, light batter, use beer instead of the milk, or milk and water. Beer batter is ideal for coating fish, prawns or vegetables.

yorkshire puddings

125 g/4 oz plain flour
pinch of salt
2 eggs
150 ml /¼ pint milk or half milk and half water
oil, for greasing

1 Make the batter as for Coating Batter (see left) and leave to stand for 30 minutes.

2 Pour ½ teaspoon oil into each of 12 deep muffin tins and place in a preheated oven, 220°C (425°F), Gas Mark 7, for 5 minutes until very hot. Quickly pour the batter into the tins to half-fill them, return them to the oven and bake for about 20 minutes until well-risen, crisp and golden brown.

MAKES: 12
PREPARATION TIME: about 10 minutes, plus standing
COOKING TIME: about 20 minutes

pancakes

225 g/4 oz plain flour
pinch of salt
1 egg, beaten
300 ml/½ pint milk or half milk and
half water
light olive oil, vegetable oil or
butter, for greasing the pan

1 Put the flour and salt into a mixing bowl and make a well in the centre. Add the egg to the well in the dry ingredients. Gradually stir in half the milk, or milk and water, then beat thoroughly until the batter is smooth and lump-free. Gradually beat in the remaining liquid until the surface is covered in tiny bubbles. Chill the batter for at least 30 minutes before using.

2 Put a little oil or butter into an 18 cm/7 inch pancake pan or heavy-based frying pan. Heat the oil until it starts to smoke – or the butter until it is foaming, but not browned. Pour off any excess oil and pour a little batter into the pan, tilting the pan until the base is coated in a thin, even layer. (If you prefer, use a small ladle to measure the batter into the pan.) Cook for 1–2 minutes until the underside of the pancake starts to turn golden.

3 Flip the pancake with a palette knife and cook for a further 30–45 seconds until it is golden on the second side. Slide the pancake out of the pan and make the remaining pancakes, oiling the pan as necessary. Set the pancakes aside while making the filling.

MAKES: 8
PREPARATION TIME: 10 minutes, plus resting
COOKING TIME: 15–25 minutes

sweet
pancakes

225 g/4 oz plain flour
pinch of salt
2 tablespoons caster sugar
1 egg, lightly beaten
300 ml/½ pint milk
25 g/1 oz unsalted butter, melted
light olive oil, vegetable oil or
butter, for greasing the pan

1 Put the flour, salt and sugar into a bowl and make a well in the centre. Pour the egg and a little of the milk into the well. Whisk the liquid, gradually incorporating the flour to make a smooth paste. Whisk in the butter, then the remaining milk until smooth. Pour the batter into a jug. Chill the batter for at least 30 minutes before using.

2 Put a little oil or butter into an 18 cm/7 inch pancake pan or heavy-based frying pan and heat until it starts to smoke. Pour off the excess oil and pour a little batter into the pan, tilting the pan until the base is coated in a thin layer. (If you prefer, use a small ladle to measure the batter into the pan.) Cook for 1–2 minutes until the underside of the pancake starts to turn golden.

3 Flip the pancake with a palette knife and cook for a further 30–45 seconds until it is golden on the second side. Slide the pancake out of the pan and make the remaining pancakes, oiling the pan as necessary. Set the pancakes aside while making the filling.

SERVES: 8–10
PREPARATION TIME: 10 minutes, plus resting
COOKING TIME: 15–25 minutes

Serving pancakes
FANS
Fold the cooked pancake in half, then fold it again into quarters, to make a fan shape. Spoon the filling between the layers of pancake.

CREPE BASKETS
Stand a number of small ovenproof bowls (one for each pancake) upside down on a baking sheet. Drape the cooked pancakes over the bowls and bake in a preheated oven, 200°C (400°F), Gas Mark 6, for about 10 minutes, until set into shape. Carefully lift the crêpe baskets off the bowls and fill with fruit, ice cream or a savoury mixture just before serving.

cheese
soufflé

50 g/2 oz butter
50 g/2 oz plain flour
250 ml/8 fl oz milk
2 tablespoons single cream
4 egg yolks
150 g/5 oz Gruyère cheese, grated
¼ teaspoon freshly grated nutmeg
5 egg whites
salt and freshly ground white
pepper

1 Make a white sauce: melt the butter in a saucepan and stir in the flour. Cook for 1–2 minutes over a low heat and then gradually add the milk, stirring well after each addition until the sauce is thick and smooth. Cook very gently for 15 minutes, stirring constantly. Remove from the heat and stir in the cream.

2 Stir in the egg yolks, a little at a time. Add the Gruyère, salt, pepper and nutmeg to taste. Beat well until the cheese melts and the mixture is smooth.

3 Whisk the egg whites in a clean bowl until they are stiff, but not dry, then fold them gently (see page 7) into the cheese sauce mixture.

4 Transfer the mixture to a greased 1.2 litre/2 pint soufflé dish. Bake in a preheated oven, 190°C (375°F), Gas Mark 5, for 15 minutes. Increase the temperature to 200°C (400°F), Gas Mark 6, and cook for a further 15 minutes until the soufflé is well risen and golden. Serve immediately.

SERVES: 4
PREPARATION TIME: 10 minutes

meringue

3 large egg whites
175 g/6 oz caster sugar
whipped cream or crème fraîche

1 Line a baking sheet with nonstick baking paper.

2 Whisk the whites in a large bowl until they form stiff peaks. Gradually whisk in about half the sugar, a tablespoonful at a time, whisking hard between each addition, until the meringue is very stiff. Lightly fold in the rest of the sugar using a metal spoon.

3 Spoon or pipe the mixture into about 12–14 rounds or ovals on to the baking sheet, then place in a preheated oven, 110°C (225°F), Gas Mark ¼ for 2–3 hours, until the meringues are crisp and dry but have not begun to turn brown.

4 Carefully lift the meringues from the paper and cool on a wire rack. Sandwich them together with whipped cream or crème fraîche.

SERVES: 6
PREPARATION TIME: 20 minutes
COOKING TIME: 2–3 hours

mayonnaise

2 egg yolks
1 teaspoon Dijon mustard
2 teaspoons lemon juice or white wine vinegar
pinch of caster sugar
300 ml/½ pint extra virgin olive oil
salt and pepper

1 Place the egg yolks, mustard, lemon juice or vinegar, sugar and salt and pepper in a bowl and whisk lightly until combined.

2 Gradually add the oil, drop by drop at first, whisking continuously until the mixture begins to thicken.

3 When the mixture has thickened slightly, add the remaining oil in a thin, steady stream, still whisking until all the oil is incorporated and the mayonnaise is thick. Taste and adjust the seasoning.

MAKES: approximately 300 ml/½ pint
PREPARATION TIME: 10 minutes

TIP If the mayonnaise starts to curdle, beat a fresh egg yolk in a bowl, then gradually whisk into the curdled mayonnaise, a spoonful at a time, until it thickens.

1 Breakfasts

eggs **benedict**

8 thick slices of cooked ham
1 tablespoon vinegar
8 eggs
4 muffins or brioche
25 g/1 oz butter
snipped chives, to garnish

Hollandaise Sauce:
3 egg yolks
1 tablespoon water
125 g/4 oz butter, softened
large pinch of salt
2 pinches cayenne pepper
1 teaspoon lemon juice
1 tablespoon single cream

1 Place the ham slices under a preheated grill and cook for 2–3 minutes on each side. Transfer to an ovenproof dish and keep warm.

2 To make the sauce, beat the egg yolks and water together in the top of a double boiler over simmering water, until the mixture is pale. Gradually add the butter, a few small pieces at a time, and continue beating until the mixture thickens. Add the salt, 1 pinch of cayenne pepper and lemon juice. Stir in the cream. Remove from the heat and keep warm.

3 Poach the eggs in a pan of gently simmering water with the vinegar for 3–4 minutes until just set.

4 Meanwhile, split and toast the muffins or brioche and spread them with the butter. Arrange on warm plates. Place a slice of ham on each muffin half and top with a poached egg. Spoon a little of the sauce over each egg. Garnish with the remaining cayenne pepper and chives and serve at once.

smoked salmon and poached egg salad on muffins

1 tablespoon vinegar

4 eggs

2 plain muffins, halved

25 g/1 oz anchovy butter

125 g/4 oz frisée lettuce, separated into leaves

250 g/8 oz smoked salmon

1 tablespoon poppy seeds

snipped chives, to garnish

Dressing:

2 teaspoons champagne or white wine vinegar

1 teaspoon Dijon mustard

1 tablespoon snipped chives

6 tablespoons extra virgin olive oil

2 ripe tomatoes, skinned, deseeded and diced

salt and pepper

1 Poach the eggs in a pan of gently simmering water with the vinegar for 3–4 minutes until just set.

2 Meanwhile, grill both sides of the muffins under a preheated grill until golden. Split the muffins and spread the insides with anchovy butter then return them to the grill for a further 1–2 minutes until golden.

3 Blend together all the dressing ingredients except the tomatoes and toss half with the frisée lettuce. Stir the diced tomato into the remaining dressing.

4 Arrange the muffins on serving plates, top each one with some of the smoked salmon, the dressed frisée and sprinkle over the poppy seeds. Carefully remove the poached eggs from the pan with a slotted spoon, drain on kitchen paper and put 1 egg on top of each muffin. Pour the tomato dressing around each muffin and serve at once, garnished with the snipped chives.

spinach and egg
muffins with
mustard hollandaise

200 g/7 oz baby spinach, washed
plenty of freshly ground nutmeg
1 tablespoon lemon juice
2 egg yolks
1 tablespoon coarse grain mustard
75 g/3 oz lightly salted butter, diced
4 plain muffins, split
1 tablespoon vinegar
4 eggs

1 Place the spinach in a saucepan with just the water that clings to the leaves and sprinkle with the nutmeg. Set aside while making the sauce.

2 Put the lemon juice, egg yolks and mustard in a heatproof bowl over a pan of gently simmering water. Add a piece of the butter and whisk until the butter has melted into the sauce. Continue whisking in the butter, a piece at a time, until the sauce is thickened and smooth. This takes about 5 minutes. If the sauce becomes too thick, whisk in a tablespoonful of hot water. Keep the sauce warm over the simmering water.

3 Toast the muffins and keep them warm. Put the vinegar in a saucepan with plenty of hot water, bring to the boil and poach the eggs. Cover the spinach pan with a lid and cook for about 2–3 minutes until the spinach has wilted. Drain and squeeze out the excess liquid.

4 Transfer the muffins to serving plates, pile them up with the spinach, then the poached eggs and top with the sauce. Serve immediately.

scrambled eggs with **manchego** and **chilli sauce**

10 eggs, beaten

1 onion, finely chopped

1 green chilli, deseeded and finely chopped, plus extra to serve

1 sweetcorn cob, kernels removed or 4 tablespoons canned sweetcorn

25 g/1 oz butter

75 g/3 oz Manchego cheese, crumbled, plus extra shavings to serve

1 tablespoon chopped coriander leaves, plus extra to serve

8 flour tortillas, warmed in the oven

snipped chives, to garnish

Sweet Chilli Sauce:

4 red chillies, deseeded and finely chopped

50 g/2 oz granulated sugar

2 tablespoons white wine vinegar

6 tablespoons water

2 tablespoons lemon juice

4½ tablespoons chopped coriander leaves

salt and pepper

If you do not have much time use ready-made chilli sauce or, for an alternative sauce, a carton of the best guacamole you can find and add a little extra chopped tomato.

1 First make the chilli sauce. Place the chopped red chillies, sugar, vinegar and water in a saucepan and heat gently until the sugar has dissolved. Bring to the boil then reduce the heat and cook for a further 10 minutes, or until it becomes thick and syrupy. Remove from the heat, allow to cool then stir in salt and pepper to taste, the lemon juice and chopped coriander.

2 To make the scrambled eggs, beat the eggs in a large bowl, add the chopped onion, green chilli and sweetcorn kernels. Season well with salt and pepper.

3 Melt the butter in a large saucepan then add the egg mixture. Cook over a moderate heat, stirring constantly, until the eggs are softly scrambled. Immediately remove the pan from the heat and stir in the Manchego and chopped coriander. Serve immediately on warm tortillas with slices of green chilli, fresh coriander and chives, plus extra shavings of Manchego and the sweet chilli sauce.

akuri

1 tablespoon butter

1 small red onion, finely chopped

1 fresh green chilli, finely sliced

8 eggs, lightly beaten

1 tablespoon crème fraîche

1 tomato, skinned and finely chopped

1 tablespoon chopped coriander leaves

sea salt

buttered toast, to serve

These spicy Indian scrambled eggs make a wonderful 'pick-me-up' breakfast or an equally good starter, served with hot buttered toast or toasted ciabatta.

1 Heat the butter in a large nonstick frying pan, add the onion and chilli and cook for 2–3 minutes.

2 Add the eggs, crème fraîche, tomato and coriander. Season with salt and cook over a low heat, stirring frequently, for about 3–4 minutes, or until the eggs are lightly scrambled and set. Serve hot with buttered toast.

breakfast **gratin**

4 tablespoons extra virgin olive oil

175 g/6 oz button mushrooms, quartered if large

1 onion, roughly chopped

4 small cooked potatoes, cubed

4 small tomatoes, halved

4 small eggs

125 g/4 oz Cheddar cheese, grated

2 tablespoons chopped chives or parsley

salt and pepper

toast, to serve

1 Heat half the oil in a large frying pan, add the mushrooms and onion and fry for 5 minutes until golden. Remove with a slotted spoon and set aside. Add the remaining oil and fry the potatoes for 5–6 minutes until golden.

2 Increase the heat, stir in the tomatoes and fry over a high heat for 2–3 minutes until lightly golden. Return the mushrooms and onions to the pan.

3 Make 4 holes in the mixture and carefully break an egg into each one. Sprinkle with the cheese and place the pan under a preheated hot grill for 4–5 minutes until the eggs are set and the cheese bubbling and golden.

4 Sprinkle with the chopped chives or parsley and serve at once with toast.

boiled eggs with
anchovy soldiers

8 anchovy fillets in oil, drained

2 tablespoons unsalted butter, softened

4 large eggs

4 thick slices white bread

pepper

cress, to serve

1 Wash the anchovies, pat dry with kitchen paper and chop finely. Beat them into the butter and season with pepper.

2 Boil the eggs for 3–4 minutes, until softly set. Meanwhile, toast the bread, butter one side with the anchovy butter, and cut into fingers.

3 Serve the eggs with the anchovy toasts and some cress.

banana **muffins**

200 g/7 oz plain white organic flour

3 teaspoons baking powder

1½ teaspoons ground cinnamon

grated nutmeg

50 g/2 oz ground almonds

50 g/2 oz soft brown sugar

2 large ripe bananas, about 350 g/11½ oz unpeeled or 250 g/8 oz peeled

2 eggs

2 tablespoons sunflower oil

125 ml/4 fl oz skimmed milk

3 tablespoons clear honey

1 Line a deep muffin tin with 10 paper cases or lightly oil the cups.

2 Sift the flour, baking powder and cinnamon into a bowl. Stir in the nutmeg, almonds and sugar.

3 Lightly mash the bananas and work in the eggs, oil, milk and honey to make a sloppy paste. Work the banana mixture into the dry ingredients, first using a fork and then folding in with a tablespoon.

4 Spoon the muffin batter into the paper cases or oiled cups and bake in a preheated oven, 190°C (375°F), Gas Mark 5, for 25 minutes (check after 20 minutes), or until well risen. When they are done, a skewer inserted in the centre should come out clean.

panettone

150 ml/¼ pint warm milk

1 tablespoon active dried yeast

about 500 g/1 lb strong plain white flour

2 teaspoons salt

1 egg, plus 4 egg yolks

75 g/3 oz caster sugar

finely grated rind of 1 lemon

finely grated rind of 1 orange

175 g/6 oz unsalted butter, softened

125 g/4 oz raisins

50 g/2 oz chopped candied orange and lemon peel

This is a classic Christmas speciality of Milan and because of the high butter content it keeps well. Start preparing it early in the day as it takes time to rise – don't be tempted to let it rise in too hot a place or the dough will be greasy. Store in the refrigerator, closely wrapped, and it will keep for up to 3 weeks.

1 Line the bottom and sides of a deep 16 cm/6½ inch cake tin with a double layer of nonstick baking parchment to project 12.5 cm/5 inches above the rim.

2 Put 4 tablespoons of the warm milk in a large bowl and mix in the yeast. Cover with a tea towel and leave in a warm place for 10 minutes until frothy. Stir in 125 g/4 oz of the flour and the remaining warm milk. Cover and leave to rise for 30 minutes.

3 Sift the remaining flour and salt on to the yeast mixture. Beat together the egg and egg yolks. Make a well in the flour and add the beaten eggs, sugar and grated lemon and orange rinds and mix to an elastic dough. Add a little more flour if necessary, but keep the dough quite soft. Work in the softened butter. Cover and leave to rise for 2–4 hours until doubled in size. Meanwhile, chop the candied peel. Knock down the dough and knead in the raisins and candied peel.

4 Put the dough in the prepared tin, cut a cross on the top with a very sharp knife, cover and leave to rise to just above the top of the tin. Bake in a preheated oven, 200°C (400°F), Gas Mark 6, for 15 minutes then lower the heat to 180°C (350°F), Gas Mark 4, and bake for about 40 minutes until well risen and golden. Leave to cool in the tin for 10 minutes then transfer to a wire rack to cool completely.

orange french toast

2 oranges
6 slices raisin bread
2 eggs
4 tablespoons milk
¼ teaspoon ground cinnamon
25 g/1 oz butter
2 tablespoons sunflower oil

To serve:
4 tablespoons full-fat crème fraîche
2 tablespoons icing sugar, sifted

1 Pare the rind from 1 of the oranges with a zester. Using a small serrated knife, peel both oranges, then cut between the membranes to separate the segments. Soak the strips of rind in iced water until they curl then drain on kitchen paper. Reserve the segments.

2 Cut the bread slices in half diagonally. Beat together the eggs, milk and cinnamon in a shallow dish. Heat half the butter and oil in a large sauté pan, then quickly dip half the bread triangles in the egg mixture, turning to cover completely, and add to pan. Cook in a single layer for 4–5 minutes, turning once, until golden on both sides. Repeat with the remaining butter and oil and bread.

3 Stack 3 triangles of bread on each serving plate, add a spoonful of crème fraîche, some orange segments and orange curls, then dust with icing sugar and serve.

fig and **molasses** cake bars

125 g/4 oz butter

50 g/2 oz unrefined raw cane caster sugar

75 ml/3 fl oz molasses

3 eggs, beaten

50 g/2 oz hazelnuts, roughly chopped

1 teaspoon vanilla extract

175 g/6 oz self-raising flour

1 teaspoon baking powder

½ teaspoon ground cinnamon

125 g/4 oz dried ready-to-eat figs or dates, roughly chopped

Molasses is a superfood. It is packed with all the B vitamins, magnesium, iron, copper and manganese and, per volume, it contains more calcium than milk. These cake bars will keep in an airtight container for 2–3 days.

1 Grease and line an 18 x 28 cm/7 x 11 inch cake tin.

2 Beat together the butter, sugar and molasses until smooth and creamy. Slowly add the beaten eggs, beating the mixture well between each addition. Add the hazelnuts, vanilla extract, flour, baking powder and cinnamon and mix thoroughly into the creamed butter.

4 Stir the figs or dates into the mixture then spoon the mixture into the prepared cake tin. Bake in a preheated oven, 180°C (350°F), Gas Mark 4, for 20–25 minutes or until firm to the touch.

5 Remove the cake from the oven and leave to cool slightly then cut it into bars. Turn out of the tin and serve.

waffles with
mixed berries

75 g/3 oz unsalted butter

2 eggs

125 ml/4 fl oz milk

125 g/4 oz self-raising wholemeal flour

3 tablespoons icing sugar, sifted

grated rind juice of ½ lemon

450 g/14½ oz pack of frozen mixed berries, defrosted

1 mint sprig, plus extra to garnish

crème fraîche, to serve

1 Melt the butter, then allow it to cool a little.

2 Separate the eggs. Add the yolks to the milk and whisk lightly. Add 1 tablespoonful of the melted butter to the milk and work in lightly with a fork.

3 Heat a waffle iron on the hob or preheat an electric one while you sift the flour into a bowl. Make a well in the flour and gradually beat in the milk and the remaining butter. Whisk the egg whites until stiff enough to hold firm peaks, then fold into the batter together with 2 tablespoons of icing sugar and the lemon rind.

4 Grease the waffle iron and pour in about one-eighth of the waffle batter. Close the lid and cook for 4–5 minutes, turning the iron once or twice if using a hob model. When the waffle is golden brown and cooked, cover and keep warm while you cook the remaining waffles.

5 Put the lemon juice and fruit into a saucepan with the mint and heat gently until the juices run, stirring to prevent the fruit sticking.

6 Put two waffles on each plate and top with some of the fruit. Shake over a little sifted icing sugar and add a mint sprig to decorate. Serve with crème fraîche.

2 Snacks
and
lunches

garlic and paprika soup
with a floating egg

4 tablespoons olive oil

12 thick slices of French bread

5 garlic cloves, sliced

1 onion, finely chopped

1 tablespoon paprika

1 teaspoon ground cumin

good pinch of saffron threads

1.2 litres/2 pints vegetable stock

25 g/1 oz dried soup pasta

4 eggs

salt and pepper

This recipe is based on a Spanish soup in which the eggs are poached or oven-baked in a rich, garlicky broth. Here, pasta is added to give a little more substance to the dish.

1 Heat the oil in a heavy-based saucepan. Add the bread and fry gently, turning once, until golden. Drain on kitchen paper.

2 Put the garlic, onion, paprika and cumin into the pan and fry gently for 3 minutes. Add the saffron and stock and bring to the boil. Stir in the soup pasta. Reduce the heat, cover the pan and simmer for about 8 minutes or until the pasta is just tender. Season to taste with salt and pepper.

3 Break the eggs one at a time on to a saucer and slide them into the pan. Cook for about 3–4 minutes until poached.

4 Arrange 3 fried bread slices in each of 4 soup bowls. Ladle the soup over the bread, making sure each serving contains an egg. Serve immediately.

egg **flower** soup

1 litre/1¾ pints chicken stock

2 spring onions, very thinly sliced on the diagonal

2 teaspoons light soy sauce

½ teaspoon sugar

2 eggs

1 teaspoon sesame oil

salt and pepper

This delicate, pretty-sounding Chinese soup sometimes goes by the name of Egg Drop Soup. It is very quick and simple to make.

1 Put the stock, spring onions, soy sauce and sugar into a large saucepan and bring to the boil.

2 Beat the eggs in a small bowl with the oil and a little salt and pepper. Pour the eggs into the boiling soup in a thin stream and break them up into threads by stirring with chopsticks or a fork. Remove the pan from the heat, cover with the lid and leave to stand for about 1 minute before serving.

caramelized onion and **emmental cheese** pancakes

8 Pancakes (see page 12)
3 tablespoons wholegrain mustard
oil or butter, for frying and greasing

Filling:
40 g/1½ oz butter
3 onions, thinly sliced
2 teaspoons caster sugar
a few thyme sprigs
200 g/7 oz Emmental or Gruyère cheese, grated
salt and black pepper

1 Make the pancakes according to the instructions on page 12 using wholemeal flour instead of plain flour and adding the wholegrain mustard. Set the pancakes aside while making the filling.

2 To make the filling, melt the butter in a heavy-based pan and fry the onions with the sugar for about 8–10 minutes until they are deep golden and caramelized. Tear the thyme leaves from the stems and add them to the pan with salt and plenty of black pepper.

3 Reserve 25 g/1 oz of the cheese and sprinkle the rest over the pancakes. Scatter the fried onions over the cheese, then roll up the pancakes and arrange them in a lightly greased, shallow ovenproof dish. Sprinkle with the reserved cheese and bake in a preheated oven, 190°C (375°F), Gas Mark 5, for about 15 minutes until the cheese has melted. Serve warm.

bacon, avocado and **soured cream** pancakes

8 Pancakes (see page 12)

250 g/8 oz thin streaky bacon rashers

2 avocados

300 ml/½ pint soured cream

1 garlic clove, crushed

3 tablespoons snipped chives

½ teaspoon mild chilli seasoning

oil, for greasing

125 g/4 oz Cheddar cheese, finely grated

salt and pepper

1 Make the pancakes according to the instructions on page 12 and keep them warm while making the filling.

2 Dry-fry the bacon in a heavy-based pan until crisp. Leave it to cool slightly then cut it into small pieces. Halve, stone and peel the avocados and slice them thinly. Mix with the bacon. Beat the soured cream with the garlic, chives, chilli powder and salt and pepper. Stir into the bacon and avocado mixture.

3 Divide the filling among the pancakes, spreading it thinly to within 1 cm/½ inch of the edge. Roll up the pancakes and place them in a lightly greased, shallow ovenproof dish.

4 Sprinkle the pancakes with the cheese and bake in a preheated oven, 190°C (375°F), Gas Mark 5, for about 20 minutes until the cheese has melted.

SERVES: 4 PREPARATION TIME: 10 minutes, plus making the pancakes
COOKING TIME: 15 minutes

buckwheat **pancakes** with **figs**, **goats' cheese** and **honey**

8 buckwheat pancakes

4 ripe figs

2 tablespoons orange juice

2 tablespoons caster sugar

125 g/4 oz soft, rindless goats' cheese

finely grated rind of 1 orange

6 tablespoons chestnut or orange blossom honey

1 Make the pancakes according to the instructions on page 12, using buckwheat flour instead of plain flour and 3 eggs instead of 1. Set the pancakes aside while making the topping.

2 Make two deep crossways cuts through each fig, leaving the figs intact at the base, and place them in a lightly greased, shallow ovenproof dish. Open the tops out slightly and sprinkle with the orange juice and 1 tablespoon of the sugar. Bake in a preheated oven, 220°C (425°F), Gas Mark 7, for 15 minutes or until lightly caramelized.

3 While the figs are cooking, wrap the pancakes in foil and put them in the oven for 10 minutes to warm through.

4 Beat the goats' cheese with the orange rind and the remaining sugar until soft. Crumple a pancake on to a warmed serving plate and top with a second crumpled pancake. Repeat with the remaining pancakes on the other serving plates. Top each one with a spoonful of the goats' cheese and a fig.

5 Stir the honey into the juices that have accumulated in the fig dish and drizzle the mixture over the pancakes.

eggs **florentine**

40 g/1½ oz butter

1 kg/2 lb fresh spinach, washed

2 large tomatoes, skinned and diced

grated nutmeg

6 large eggs

150 ml/¼ pint crème fraîche

50 ml/2 fl oz double cream

40 g/1½ oz Cheddar cheese, grated

40 g/1½ oz Parmesan cheese, freshly grated

salt and pepper

1 Melt half the butter in a large saucepan. Add the spinach with just the water that clings to the leaves, cover and cook gently until wilted and soft. Drain well and squeeze out the water. Return the spinach to the pan, add the tomatoes and season with nutmeg and salt and pepper.

2 Grease 6 175 ml/6 fl oz gratin dishes with the remaining butter. Divide the spinach among the dishes, making a well in the centre of each one for an egg and leaving a 1 cm/½ inch space between the spinach and the rim of the dish.

3 Break an egg into the centre of each gratin dish and dust with salt and pepper. Mix together the crème fraîche and cream. Spoon evenly over the eggs and sprinkle with the Cheddar and Parmesan.

4 Set the gratin dishes on a heavy baking sheet and bake in a preheated oven, 220°C (425°F), Gas Mark 7, for about 10–12 minutes, until the whites are set but the yolks are still runny.

5 Remove the dishes from the oven and place under a preheated hot grill until the topping is bubbling and the cheese golden brown. Serve immediately.

deep-fried **gnocchi** with **salsa rossa**

Salsa Rossa:
7 very ripe tomatoes, chopped
1 carrot, finely chopped
2 onions, finely chopped
3 garlic cloves, finely chopped
1 small dried red chilli, deseeded
3 tablespoons granulated sugar
1 tablespoon red wine vinegar
about 1 tablespoon olive oil
salt and pepper

Gnocchi:
500 ml/17 fl oz milk
250 g/8 oz semolina
75 g/3 oz Parmesan cheese, freshly grated
50 g/2 oz butter
1 egg yolk
pinch of chilli powder
grated nutmeg
plain flour, for coating
2 eggs, beaten
dry breadcrumbs, for coating
oil, for deep-frying
salt and pepper

The secret of this sauce from Piedmont lies in its long, slow cooking. It is rich and concentrated, and slightly sweet and sour – perfect for dipping these crisp deep-fried snacks with their soft cheesy centres.

1 To make the sauce, put the tomatoes, carrot, onions, garlic, chilli, sugar and vinegar into a heavy saucepan with the olive oil. Bring to the boil, then turn down the heat, cover the pan and simmer for 2–3 hours until the sauce is very soft.

2 To make the gnocchi, pour the milk into a saucepan and whisk in the semolina. Bring the mixture slowly to the boil, stirring all the time until it really thickens – about 10 minutes.

3 Beat in the Parmesan, butter, egg yolk, chilli and plenty of nutmeg. Taste and season well with salt and pepper. Line a baking sheet or Swiss roll tin with clingfilm and spread out the mixture to a depth of 1 cm/½ inch. Leave to cool then chill in the refrigerator for about 2 hours.

4 When the sauce is ready, remove and discard the chilli and blend the sauce in a food processor or pass through a fine sieve. Taste and season with salt and pepper and a little extra olive oil. Reheat the salsa rossa to serve with the gnocchi.

5 When the gnocchi is well chilled and set, cut into bite-sized triangles with a wet knife. Dip each triangle in flour, then in the beaten egg and finally in the breadcrumbs. Heat the oil to 180°C/350°F or until a cube of bread browns in 30 seconds, then deep-fry the gnocchi in batches for about 2–3 minutes until golden and crisp. Sprinkle with salt. Allow to cool slightly then serve with the salsa rossa.

lemon-scented **spinach** and **ricotta** gnocchi

625 g/1¼ lb fresh spinach, washed

25 g/1 oz butter

1 shallot, finely chopped

finely grated rind of 1 lemon

150 g/5 oz fresh ricotta, sieved

75 g/3 oz plain white flour

2 egg yolks

75 g/3 oz Parmesan cheese, freshly grated, plus extra to serve

grated nutmeg

semolina flour or plain flour, for sprinkling

salt and pepper

herb sprigs, to garnish

Sauce:

2 lemons

175 g/6 oz unsalted butter

2 bay leaves

1 Place the spinach in a saucepan with minimal water and cook until wilted. Allow to cool slightly, then squeeze out most of the moisture. Roughly chop and set aside.

2 Melt the butter and fry the shallot until golden. Stir in the spinach and lemon rind, and cook for a couple of minutes until the spinach is coated and mixed with the butter and shallot. Tip into a large bowl. Beat in the ricotta, flour, egg yolks and Parmesan. When thoroughly mixed, taste and season well with nutmeg and salt and pepper. Cover and leave to stand in the refrigerator for at least a couple of hours.

3 To make the sauce, scrub the lemons under hot water. Thinly pare the rind from both lemons, avoiding the bitter white pith. Squeeze the juice from 1 lemon and reserve. Melt the butter in a small pan. Add the lemon rind and bay leaves and heat gently for 2 minutes then remove the pan from the heat and leave the sauce in a warm place to infuse for at least 1 hour (the longer this can be left the better).

4 Take large teaspoonfuls of the gnocchi mixture and quickly roll into cork shapes. Place on a tray lined with a tea towel sprinkled with semolina flour or plain flour.

5 Reheat the butter and strain it into a clean pan. Stir in the lemon juice, bring to the boil and season with salt and pepper. Spoon a third of the sauce into a warmed shallow serving dish.

6 Bring a large pan of salted water to the boil. Drop in all the gnocchi at once and cook them for 2–3 minutes after the water returns to the boil. Lift out with a slotted spoon, drain well and transfer to the warmed dish. Pour over the rest of the lemony butter and serve with freshly grated Parmesan. Garnish with herb sprigs.

baked **ricotta cheeses** with **bay** leaves

4 sun-dried tomatoes (the dried
variety)

500 g/1 lb drained ricotta cheese

3 large eggs

12 oven-dried black olives, pitted
and roughly chopped

2 tablespoons salted capers, rinsed
and chopped, plus extra to garnish

a little butter

18 fresh young bay leaves

salt and pepper

To serve:
olive oil
rocket leaves

These little savoury cheesecakes are permeated with the musky perfume of
fresh bay leaves, a much-loved flavouring in Sicily. Choose soft young leaves
that will bend to fit your moulds – the smell as they bake is wonderful. Serve
at room temperature with just a drizzle of olive oil and some black pepper.

1 Soak the sun-dried tomatoes in warm water for 10 minutes. Pat dry and then
shred finely.

2 Push the ricotta through a sieve into a bowl. Beat in the eggs, then lightly stir in
the sun-dried tomatoes, olives and capers. Taste and season very well.

3 Generously butter 6 125 ml/4 fl oz ramekins or moulds. Place a bay leaf at the
bottom of each one, and two around the side. Chill the ramekins to set the butter
and keep the bay leaves in place. Spoon in the ricotta mixture and level it with a palette
knife. Set the ramekins on a baking sheet.

4 Bake the cheeses in a preheated oven, 190°C (375°F), Gas Mark 5, for 20 minutes
until set. Remove them from the oven, leave to cool, then chill. Turn out the
cheeses and serve at room temperature with a drizzle of olive oil, a few rocket leaves
and some extra capers. The bay leaves should not be eaten.

quick pasta **carbonara**

400 g/13 oz dried spaghetti or other long thin pasta

2 tablespoons olive oil

1 onion, finely chopped

200 g/7 oz pancetta or streaky bacon rashers, diced

2 garlic cloves, finely chopped

3 eggs

4 tablespoons grated Parmesan cheese

3 tablespoons chopped flat leaf parsley

3 tablespoons single cream

salt and pepper

green salad, to serve (optional)

1 Cook the pasta in a large saucepan of boiling salted water for 8–10 minutes or according to the packet instructions, until al dente – tender but with bite.

2 Meanwhile, heat the oil in a large nonstick frying pan. Add the onion and fry until it is soft. Then add the pancetta or bacon and the garlic, and cook gently for 4–5 minutes.

3 Beat the eggs with the Parmesan, parsley and cream. Season with salt and pepper to taste and set aside.

4 Drain the pasta and add it to the onion and pancetta. Stir over a gentle heat until combined, then pour in the egg mixture. Stir and remove the pan from the heat. Continue mixing well for a few seconds, until the eggs are lightly cooked and creamy, then serve immediately. A green salad goes well with creamy carbonara.

spanish omelette

150 ml/¼ pint olive oil
4 large potatoes, cut into 3 mm/
⅛ inch slices
1 large onion, thinly sliced
4–5 large eggs
salt and pepper

This thick, juicy, fragrant omelette, known as a tortilla in Spain, can be served hot (though more generally warm) or cold. It can be a first course, main course, light supper or snack, and is both delicious and satisfying.

1 Heat the oil in a 20–23 cm/8–9 inch heavy nonstick frying pan. Add the potatoes and onion, cover the pan and cook over a low heat without colouring, until the potatoes are tender, lifting and turning them occasionally. This will take about 30 minutes.

2 Beat the eggs until they are slightly foamy. Season with salt and pepper. Once the vegetables are soft and well cooked, lift them out of the pan with a slotted spoon and drain them in a colander. Reserve the oil. Add the potatoes and onion to the beaten eggs, pressing them well down so that they are completely covered. If possible, leave to stand for about 15 minutes.

3 Wipe the pan clean, then heat about 2–3 tablespoons of the reserved oil. Add the egg mixture and quickly spread it out with a palette knife. Reduce the heat and cook very gently, shaking the pan occasionally to prevent it from sticking. When the mixture begins to brown underneath and shrink slightly from the edge of the pan, after about 15 minutes, remove the pan from the heat.

4 Turn the tortilla over by placing a flat plate, slightly larger than the pan, on top of it and quickly turn the tortilla upside down on to the plate. Heat another tablespoon of oil in the pan, then slide the tortilla back to brown the other side. This will take another 3–4 minutes. Alternatively, just slip the pan under a preheated moderate grill and cook until the surface is golden brown. The tortilla should be golden brown on the outside and moist and juicy inside. Transfer to a plate and serve hot or cold.

courgette and **mint** frittata

2 tablespoons olive oil

1 red onion, thinly sliced

500 g/1 lb courgettes, thinly sliced

1 red chilli, deseeded and thinly sliced

5 eggs, beaten

1 tablespoon double cream

4 tablespoons chopped mint

50 g/2 oz Parmesan cheese, grated

salt and pepper

grilled foccacia bread or warmed crusty bread, to serve

A frittata is an Italian set omelette which may be served warm or cold.

1 Heat the oil in a 20 cm/8 inch frying pan. Add the onion and cook over a moderate heat for 3–4 minutes, stirring, until slightly softened. Add the courgettes and chilli, then increase the heat to high and cook for 4–5 minutes.

2 Beat the eggs with the cream, adding the mint and salt and pepper to taste. Pour the eggs over the courgette mixture. Reduce the heat and cook the frittata for about 5 minutes or until it is just set on top and golden underneath. Use a spatula or fish slice to lift the edge of the mixture to check that it is browned underneath.

3 Sprinkle the Parmesan over the frittata and place it under a preheated hot grill for 2–3 minutes or until the frittata is golden and set.

4 Serve the frittata cut into wedges, on grilled foccacia bread, or with thick slices of warmed crusty bread.

fresh **pea** and **tomato** frittata

2 tablespoons extra virgin olive oil
1 bunch spring onions, sliced
1 garlic clove, crushed
125 g/4 oz cherry tomatoes, halved
125 g/4 oz frozen peas
6 eggs
2 tablespoons chopped mint
a handful pea shoots (optional)
salt and pepper

To serve:
rocket leaves
Parmesan cheese shavings (optional)

1 Heat the oil in a nonstick frying pan and fry the spring onions and garlic for 2 minutes, then add the tomatoes and peas.

2 Beat the eggs with the mint and season with salt and pepper. Swirl the egg mixture into the pan, scatter over the pea shoots, if using, and cook over a moderate heat for 3–4 minutes, or until almost set.

3 Transfer the pan to a preheated grill and cook for 2–3 minutes longer, or until lightly browned and cooked through. Allow to cool slightly then serve in wedges with the rocket and Parmesan shavings, if liked.

cauliflower, ginger and saffron frittata

4 tablespoons milk

¼ teaspoon saffron threads

1 teaspoon sesame oil

8 large eggs, beaten

½ teaspoon salt

2 tablespoons chopped coriander leaves

2 tablespoons vegetable oil

1 leek, trimmed, cleaned and sliced

1 tablespoon grated root ginger

1 small cauliflower (about 375 g/ 12 oz), divided into small florets

1 tablespoon sesame seeds

1 Warm the milk and saffron threads in a saucepan until almost boiling. Remove from the heat, add the sesame oil and set aside for 10 minutes to infuse. Beat in the eggs, salt and coriander.

2 Heat the vegetable oil in a large heavy-based nonstick frying pan. Add the leek, ginger and cauliflower and fry over a moderate heat for 10 minutes until the vegetables are lightly golden.

3 Stir in the egg mixture until evenly combined and cook over a moderate heat for 8–10 minutes until the frittata is almost set. Sprinkle over the sesame seeds.

4 Place the pan under a preheated grill and cook for 3–4 minutes until browned on the top. Cool slightly, carefully remove the frittata from the pan, cut into wedges and serve immediately.

country **salad** with **horseradish** dressing

2 eggs
250 g/8 oz shelled broad beans
125 g/4 oz green beans, halved
500 g/1 lb firm ripe plum tomatoes, cut into wedges
½ small cucumber, sliced thickly
2 celery sticks, sliced
175 g/6 oz cooked beetroot, sliced
1 small red onion, sliced thinly
2 tablespoons drained capers
salt

Dressing:
2 tablespoons grated horseradish or 1 tablespoon creamed horseradish
4 tablespoons extra virgin olive oil
2 teaspoons red wine vinegar
pinch of sugar
2 tablespoons chopped fresh mixed herbs
salt and pepper

1 Hard-boil the eggs according to the instructions on page 7, then cool in cold water.

2 Blanch the broad beans in boiling salted water for 3 minutes then drain, refresh under cold water and pat dry on kitchen paper. Remove and discard the tough outer skin. Blanch the green beans for 3 minutes, drain, refresh under cold water and pat dry on kitchen paper.

3 Place the broad beans and green beans in a large bowl and add the tomatoes, cucumber, celery, beetroot, onion and capers.

4 To make the dressing, mix together the horseradish, olive oil, vinegar, sugar and herbs and season to taste with salt and pepper. Pour over the salad and toss gently until all the ingredients are evenly coated. Transfer the salad to a serving dish and top with the eggs, cut lengthways into quarters. Serve at once.

thai **egg salad** with crispy **basil**

4 eggs
3 shallots, finely sliced
5 small fresh green chillies, finely chopped
1 large garlic clove, finely sliced
juice of 2 limes
2 tablespoons Thai fish sauce or soy sauce
½ teaspoon sugar
groundnut oil, for frying
25–50 g/1–2 oz basil leaves

1 Hard-boil the eggs according to the instructions on page 7. Shell the eggs and cut them in half lengthways.

2 Put the eggs, yolk side up, on a serving dish or in a bowl and sprinkle the shallots over them. In a small bowl, put the chillies, garlic, lime juice, fish or soy sauce and sugar and mix together well. Spoon the mixture over the eggs.

3 Heat some oil in a wok, throw in the basil leaves and watch them become crispy. Quickly remove them from the oil with a slotted spoon and drain on kitchen paper. Scatter over the salad and serve.

thai egg strips

3 eggs, beaten

1 shallot, finely sliced

green shoots of 1 spring onion, sliced

1–2 small fresh red chillies, finely chopped

1 tablespoon chopped coriander leaves

1 tablespoon groundnut oil

salt and pepper

julienne of spring onion, to garnish (optional)

This classic Thai snack makes an excellent nibble to serve with drinks.

1 Mix all the ingredients, except the oil and the garnish, in a bowl.

2 Heat the oil in a frying pan or wok, pour in the egg mixture and swirl it around the pan to produce a large thin omelette. Cook for 1–2 minutes until firm.

3 Slide the omelette out on to a plate and roll it up as though it were a pancake. Allow to cool.

4 When the omelette is cool, cut the roll crossways into 5 mm/¼ inch or 1 cm/½ inch sections, depending on how wide you want your strips to be. Serve them still rolled up or straightened out, in a heap. Garnish with strips of spring onion, if liked.

poached eggs with **parma ham** and **herb tomatoes**

4 ripe tomatoes
2 tablespoons chopped basil
4 tablespoons extra virgin olive oil
4 slices Parma ham
1 tablespoon vinegar
4 large eggs
salt and pepper
hot buttered plain muffins, to serve

This delicious combination is a healthier version of a traditional 'fry-up'.

1 Halve the tomatoes and place, cut-side up, on a grill pan. Mix the basil with 2 tablespoons of the oil and drizzle over the cut tomatoes. Season well with salt and pepper. Cook under a preheated grill for about 6–7 minutes, until softened. Remove and keep warm.

2 Meanwhile, heat the remaining oil in a frying pan and fry the Parma ham until crisp. Drain on kitchen paper and keep warm.

3 Poach the eggs in a pan of gently simmering water with the vinegar for 3–4 minutes until just set. Serve on buttered toasted muffins with the ham and grilled tomatoes.

smoked **haddock**, poached eggs and **caper** butter

**4 smoked haddock fillets, about
175 g/6 oz each**

4 eggs

50 g/2 oz unsalted butter, softened

**2 tablespoons capers in brine,
drained and rinsed**

6 dill sprigs

salt and pepper

1 Put the haddock into a frying pan, skin-side up, and cover with cold water. Bring to the boil and poach for 5 minutes, then remove with a slotted spoon and drain on kitchen paper. Set aside and keep warm. Reserve the fish cooking liquid.

2 Crack the eggs into the cooking liquid and poach for 3–4 minutes until just set.

3 To make the caper butter, melt the butter in a small frying pan until foaming. Add the capers and dill and fry until the butter starts to turn brown. Season to taste with salt and pepper.

4 To serve, top each haddock fillet with a poached egg and drizzle with some of the caper butter.

chickpea purée with eggs and **spiced oil**

425 g/14 oz can chickpeas, rinsed and drained

3 garlic cloves, sliced

4 tablespoons tahini

4 tablespoons milk

5 tablespoons olive oil

4 teaspoons lemon juice

2 eggs

½ teaspoon each of cumin, coriander and fennel seeds, lightly crushed

1 teaspoon sesame seeds

¼ teaspoon chilli flakes

good pinch of ground turmeric

salt and pepper

coriander leaves, to garnish

Smooth chickpea purée, topped with fried eggs and spicy oil, makes a great snack at any time of the day. Serve any leftover purée just as you would hummus, with warm pitta bread.

1 Place the chickpeas in a food processor or blender with the garlic, tahini, milk, 2 tablespoons of the oil and 3 teaspoons of the lemon juice. Season to taste with salt and pepper and process until smooth, scraping the mixture from around the sides of the bowl halfway through. Transfer to a small heavy-based saucepan and heat through gently for about 3 minutes while preparing the eggs.

2 Heat another tablespoon of the oil in a small frying pan and fry the eggs. Pile the chickpea purée on to serving plates and top each mound with an egg.

3 Add the remaining oil and the spices to the pan and heat through gently for 1 minute. Season lightly with salt and pepper and stir in the remaining lemon juice. Pour over the eggs and serve garnished with coriander leaves.

green lentils with egg and **spiced mayonnaise**

4 eggs

200 g/7 oz dried green lentils or
425 g/14 oz can green lentils

4 spring onions, finely chopped

2 tablespoons chopped coriander
leaves

1 tablespoon olive oil

1 teaspoon lemon or lime juice

salt and pepper

fine strips of red chilli, to garnish

Dressing:
6 tablespoons Mayonnaise (see
page 15)

1–2 tablespoons mild curry paste

This salad makes a good starter or light lunch served with garlic naan bread. Don't overcook the eggs as they are best if the yolks are slightly creamy.

1 If using dried lentils, cook them according to the packet instructions and put to one side.

2 Hard-boil the eggs according to the instructions on page 7, then cool in cold water.

3 Rinse the cooked or canned lentils and drain thoroughly. Place in a bowl with the spring onions, coriander, olive oil and lemon or lime juice. Season with salt and pepper and mix well.

4 To make the dressing, stir together the mayonnaise and mild curry paste until smooth.

5 To serve the salad, arrange piles of the lentil mixture on 4 individual plates. Top each serving with a dollop of dressing and an egg, halved or sliced. Garnish each serving with a few strips of red chilli.

piroshki

Dough:
250 g/8 oz plain flour
½ teaspoon salt
2 teaspoons fast-acting dried yeast
1 teaspoon sugar
50–75 ml/2–3 fl oz warm milk
1 small egg, beaten
25 g/1 oz melted butter

Filling:
15 g/½ oz dried ceps
25 g/1 oz butter
4 large spring onions, finely chopped
2 garlic cloves, crushed
250 g/8 oz chestnut mushrooms, finely chopped
2 tablespoons chopped dill
50 g/2 oz cooked rice
2 eggs
2 tablespoons soured cream
salt and pepper

Egg Glaze:
1 small egg
1 tablespoon milk

1 First make the dough. Sift the flour and salt into a bowl and stir in the yeast and sugar. Make a well in the centre and gradually work in the milk, egg and butter to form a soft, slightly sticky dough. Turn out and knead on a lightly floured surface for 10 minutes until the dough is smooth and elastic. Cover the bowl with clingfilm and leave to rise in a warm place until doubled in size, about 1½–2 hours.

2 To make the filling, soak the dried ceps in 150 ml/¼ pint boiling water for 30 minutes. Drain and reserve the liquid; chop and reserve the ceps. Hard-boil the eggs according to the instructions on page 7, then cool in cold water.

3 Melt the butter in a frying pan and fry the spring onions and garlic for 5 minutes. Add the ceps and chestnut mushrooms and continue to fry over a high heat for 5–6 minutes until the mushrooms are golden. Add the reserved cep liquid and boil until it has almost evaporated. Transfer to a bowl, stir in the dill, rice, soured cream and hard-boiled eggs (finely chopped) and season to taste. Set aside to cool.

4 Knock back the dough and then divide it into 14 balls. Roll out each one on a lightly floured surface to a 10 cm/4 inch round.

5 To make the egg glaze, beat together the egg and milk and season with a pinch of salt.

6 Put a spoonful of the mushroom filling in the centre of each round. Brush the edges with egg glaze, pull up the sides and pinch together across the centre to seal in the filling (like a Cornish pasty). Transfer the piroshki to lightly greased baking sheets, cover loosely with greased clingfilm and leave to rise for a further 20–30 minutes.

7 Bake in a preheated oven, 200°C (400°F), Gas Mark 6, for 15–20 minutes until risen and golden. Allow to cool for about 10 minutes. Serve warm.

★ If using a food processor, sift the flour and salt into the bowl and stir in the yeast and sugar. Gradually blend in the milk, egg and butter with a dough hook on a low setting. Knead for 10 minutes. Leave to rise as instructed in step 1.

griddled **asparagus** with frazzled eggs and **parmesan**

500 g/1 lb thin asparagus, trimmed
olive oil, for frying
4 fresh eggs, chilled
salt and pepper
Parmesan shavings, to serve

Fresh young asparagus tastes wonderful with eggs in any form. These eggs are fried in very hot olive oil, which gives them a crisp, brown lacy edge but a soft yolk.

1 Blanch the asparagus for 2 minutes in salted boiling water. Drain and refresh under cold water. Drain again and toss in a little olive oil, to coat.

2 Cook the asparagus on a preheated griddle or under a preheated grill for 2–3 minutes on each side until tender but still with a bite. Set aside to cool slightly.

3 Pour enough olive oil into a large frying pan to coat the base generously and heat until almost smoking. Crack each egg into a cup and carefully slide into the pan. Watch out as the oil will splutter! Once the edges of the eggs have bubbled up and browned, turn the heat right down and cover the pan with a lid. Leave for about 1 minute, then lift out the eggs and drain them on kitchen paper. The yolks should have formed a skin but remain runny underneath.

4 Divide the asparagus among 4 warmed plates and top each pile with an egg. Sprinkle with black pepper and Parmesan shavings. Serve with a little pot of salt for the eggs.

quails' eggs with spiced salt

24 quails' eggs
1 teaspoon Szechuan peppercorns
2 tablespoons sea salt
½ teaspoon Chinese five-spice powder

Szechuan peppercorns, also known as farchiew and anise pepper, are not really pepper, but the dried red berries of a type of ash tree. Nevertheless, they have a hot, peppery flavour, which is best brought out by dry-roasting in a cast-iron frying pan.

1 Cook the eggs in a pan of gently simmering water for 3 minutes. Plunge them into cold water.

2 Dry-fry the peppercorns until they are smoking. Cool and grind to a powder with the salt. Stir in the five-spice powder.

3 Shell the eggs and serve with a bowl of the spiced salt, to dip.

smoked **salmon** and **quails' egg** salad

250 g/8 oz small new potatoes

about 250 g/8 oz mixed salad leaves (frisée, rocket, lamb's lettuce, escarole, salad burnet)

2–3 tablespoons croûtons

1 teaspoon white wine vinegar

12 quails' eggs

125 g/4 oz smoked salmon, cut into strips

2 tablespoons snipped chives

salt and pepper

Dressing:

5 tablespoons Mayonnaise (see page 15)

1 tablespoon lemon juice

3–4 tablespoons water

Quails' eggs and smoked salmon make this a rather special salad. If you prefer you can substitute hens' eggs – use 4 eggs, poached for 5 minutes, or gently fried in butter until just set.

1 Bring a saucepan of water to the boil, add the potatoes and cook for about 10 minutes, or until just tender. Drain in a colander and refresh under cold running water. Drain again thoroughly. Allow to cool completely, then cut the potatoes into halves or quarters.

2 To make the dressing, mix together the mayonnaise, lemon juice and water.

3 Shortly before serving, arrange the salad leaves in a large shallow serving dish or on individual plates. Scatter the croûtons over the top.

4 Bring a frying pan of water to simmering point. Add the vinegar. Carefully break in 6 of the eggs and poach for about 3–4 minutes. Using a slotted spoon, transfer the poached eggs to a plate and repeat with the rest of the eggs. Alternatively, fry the eggs in butter until just firm.

5 Arrange the cooked quails' eggs and salmon strips on the salad and scatter over the chives. Add salt and pepper to taste. Drizzle over the dressing or serve separately.

3 Dinner

courgette, sun-dried tomato and ricotta flan

Shortcrust Pastry:

175 g/6 oz plain flour, plus extra for dusting

pinch of salt

75 g/3 oz butter, diced

2–3 tablespoons cold water

Filling:

2 tablespoons extra virgin olive oil

1 small onion, thinly sliced thinly

2 courgettes, thinly sliced

50 g/2 oz drained sun-dried tomatoes in oil, sliced

250 g/8 oz ricotta or curd cheese

2 tablespoons milk

2 eggs, beaten

4 tablespoons chopped fresh herbs (basil, rosemary, sage, thyme)

12 black olives, pitted and halved

salt and pepper

1 To make the pastry, sift the flour and salt into a bowl and rub in the butter until the mixture resembles fine breadcrumbs. Gradually work in enough water to form a soft dough. On a lightly floured surface, knead the dough until smooth, then wrap in clingfilm and chill for 30 minutes.

2 On a lightly floured surface, roll out the pastry and use to line a 23 cm/9 inch flan tin. Prick the base with a fork and chill for 20 minutes. Line the pastry case with foil and baking beans and cook in a preheated oven, 200°C (400°F), Gas Mark 6, for 10 minutes. Remove the foil and beans and bake for a further 10–12 minutes until the pastry is crisp and golden.

3 Heat the oil in a frying pan, add the onion and courgettes and fry gently for 5–6 minutes until lightly golden. Scatter over the base of the pastry case and top with the sun-dried tomatoes.

4 Beat together the ricotta, milk, eggs, herbs and salt and pepper and spread over the courgette mixture. Scatter over the olives and bake for 30–35 minutes until firm and golden.

french **onion** flan

Shortcrust Pastry:
250 g/8 oz plain flour, plus extra for dusting
pinch of salt
50 g/2 oz butter
3 tablespoons cold water

Filling:
50 g/2 oz butter
500 g/1 lb onions, thinly sliced
2 teaspoons tomato purée
3 eggs
150 ml/¼ pint milk
salt and pepper

1 To make the pastry, sift the flour and salt into a bowl and rub in the butter until the mixture resembles fine breadcrumbs. Gradually work in enough water to form a soft dough. On a lightly floured surface, knead the dough until smooth, then wrap in clingfilm and chill for 30 minutes.

2 Meanwhile, melt half of the butter in a frying pan. Add the onions with the tomato purée, season lightly with salt and pepper and stir well. Cook over a low heat, stirring occasionally, for 15 minutes. Remove from the heat and leave to cool.

3 Roll out the pastry on a lightly floured surface and use to line a 25 cm/10 inch loose-bottomed fluted flan tin set on a baking sheet. Prick the base with a fork.

4 Line the pastry-lined tin with foil and fill with baking beans. Bake blind in a preheated oven, 200°C (400°F), Gas Mark 6, for 15 minutes. Remove the paper and beans and return the flan case to the oven for a further 10–15 minutes until the pastry is dry and the flan case is cooked through. Remove from the oven.

5 Arrange the onions in the flan case. Beat the eggs with the milk in a bowl and add salt and pepper to taste. Strain into the flan case. Lower the oven temperature to 180°C (350°F), Gas Mark 4 and bake the flan for 30–35 minutes until the filling is set and lightly golden. Serve hot or cold.

hazelnut and gorgonzola quiche

Cheese Pastry:

250 g/8 oz plain flour

pinch of salt

pinch of cayenne pepper

75 g/3 oz butter

25 g/1 oz Cheddar cheese, finely grated

6–8 tablespoons cold water

Filling:

50 g/2 oz butter

1 tablespoon vegetable oil

2 large leeks, thinly sliced

150 ml/¼ pint whipping cream

150 ml/¼ pint milk

2 tablespoons chopped flat leaf parsley

2 eggs, beaten

125 g/4 oz Gorgonzola cheese, crumbled

75 g/3 oz whole hazelnuts, lightly toasted

salt and pepper

1 First make the cheese pastry. Put the flour, salt and cayenne pepper in a mixing bowl or food processor or blender with the butter and work to fine breadcrumbs. Add the grated Cheddar and mix together. Add the cold water and combine the ingredients to make a soft, pliable pastry. Wrap in clingfilm and chill for 1 hour.

2 Roll out the pastry on a lightly floured surface and use to line a deep 20 cm/8 inch flan tin. Prick the base with a fork and chill for 1 hour. Line the pastry case with foil and fill with baking beans. Bake blind in a preheated oven, 190°C (375°F), Gas Mark 5, for 12 minutes. Remove the foil and baking beans and bake for a further 5 minutes. Remove from the oven, but leave the oven on.

3 To make the filling, heat the butter and oil in a large frying pan and fry the sliced leeks until softened and caramelized. Remove from the heat and allow to cool.

4 Beat together the cream, milk, chopped parsley and eggs. Stir the egg mixture into the caramelized leeks and season well with salt and pepper. Stir the crumbled Gorgonzola into the mixture, then pour it into the cooked pastry case. Smooth the surface, then scatter the hazelnuts over the top.

5 Bake the quiche in the oven for 40–50 minutes, or until the egg mixture has just set in the middle. Remove from the oven and allow to cool slightly then serve with a mixed green salad.

spinach and feta filo pie with pine nuts

750 g/1½ lb fresh spinach, washed

250 g/8 oz feta cheese, roughly crumbled

½ teaspoon dried chilli flakes

75 g/3 oz Parmesan, freshly grated

50 g/2 oz pine nuts, toasted

15 g/½ oz dill, chopped

15 g/½ oz tarragon, chopped

3 eggs, beaten

1 teaspoon grated nutmeg

250 g/8 oz fresh filo pastry

5–8 tablespoons olive oil

1 tablespoon sesame seeds

salt and pepper

1 Put the spinach into a large saucepan with just the water that clings to the leaves and cook gently until wilted and soft. Drain well then squeeze out the water.

2 Mix the feta into the spinach with the chilli flakes, Parmesan, pine nuts, dill and tarragon. Add the beaten eggs to the mixture with plenty of salt and pepper and the grated nutmeg. Mix well.

3 Unwrap the filo pastry and, working quickly, brush the top sheet of pastry with a little olive oil. (While working, keep the stack of filo pastry covered with a clean tea towel to prevent it from drying out.) Lay the sheet in the bottom of a lightly greased 20 cm/8 inch loose-bottomed cake tin with the edges overlapping the rim of the tin. Brush the next sheet of pastry and lay it in the opposite direction from the first sheet to completely cover the base of the tin. Repeat this brushing with oil and layering in the tin until 6–8 sheets of pastry have created a shell and there are at least 3 sheets of pastry left for a lid.

4 Spoon the spinach mixture into the filo pastry shell, pushing it in well with the back of the spoon and levelling the surface.

5 Brush the next sheet of pastry with oil and then cut the length of the remaining stack of filo pastry into 5 cm/2 inch wide strips. One by one, place these strips of pastry over the top of the spinach in a casual folded arrangement, remembering to brush all the strips of pastry with oil.

6 Once all the strips are in place, fold in the over-hanging filo towards the middle. Sprinkle with sesame seeds and bake in a preheated oven, 190°C (375°F), Gas Mark 5, for 1 hour. Remove from the oven, leave to cool for 15 minutes, then gently push the pie up and out of the tin. Serve warm or cold.

munster, red pepper and chive tartlets

Shortcrust Pastry:
400 g/13 oz plain flour, plus extra for dusting
½ teaspoon salt
200 g/7 oz butter
6 tablespoons cold water

Filling:
1 tablespoon vegetable oil
15 g/½ oz butter
1 red onion, finely chopped
1 small red pepper, roasted, peeled and thinly sliced
150 ml/¼ pint single cream
2 eggs
2 garlic cloves, crushed
15 g/½ oz chives, snipped
75 g/3 oz) Munster cheese, roughly chopped
salt and pepper
basil leaves, to garnish

1 To make the pastry, sift the flour and salt into a bowl and rub in the butter until the mixture resembles fine breadcrumbs. Gradually work in enough water to form a soft dough. On a lightly floured surface, knead the dough until smooth, then wrap in clingfilm and chill for 30 minutes.

2 Roll out the pastry on a lightly floured surface and use to line 4 10 cm/4 inch tartlet tins. Prick the bases, line with circles of greaseproof paper and fill with baking beans, then chill for 30 minutes.

3 Place the tartlets on a baking sheet and bake blind in a preheated oven, 190°C (375°F), Gas Mark 5, for 8 minutes. Remove the paper and beans and bake for a further 2–3 minutes, or until the shells are crisp and beginning to brown. Remove from the oven and cool slightly. Leave the oven on.

4 Heat the oil and butter in a pan and fry the sliced red onion until caramelized. Divide the onion and the roasted red pepper strips among the pastry shells.

5 Beat together the cream, eggs and salt and pepper. Add the crushed garlic and chives to the mixture and divide it among the pastry shells. Sprinkle the Munster over the tartlets and bake in the oven for 20–25 minutes, or until just cooked. Garnish with basil.

herb roulade with
spinach and ricotta

25 g/1 oz butter
40 g/1½ oz plain flour
1 teaspoon Dijon mustard
200 ml/7 fl oz semi-skimmed milk
50 g/2 oz vegetarian cheese, grated
4 eggs, separated
4 tablespoons chopped fresh mixed
herbs (basil, chervil, chives, tarragon,
thyme)
salt and pepper

Fresh Tomato Sauce:
1 kg/2 lb ripe tomatoes, roughly
chopped
2 tablespoons extra virgin olive oil
2 garlic cloves, chopped
2 tablespoons chopped basil
1 teaspoon grated lemon rind
pinch of sugar
salt and pepper

Filling:
175 g/6 oz ricotta or curd cheese
2 tablespoons extra virgin olive oil,
plus extra for oiling
pinch of grated nutmeg
1 leek, finely chopped
750 g/1½ lb fresh spinach
¼ teaspoon grated nutmeg

1 To make the fresh tomato sauce, place all the ingredients in a saucepan and bring to the boil. Cover and simmer gently for 30 minutes. Remove the lid and simmer gently for 20 minutes until the sauce is thick.

2 Meanwhile, grease a 23 x 33 cm/9 x 13 inch Swiss roll tin and line with nonstick baking paper. Melt the butter in a saucepan, stir in the flour and mustard and cook over a low heat for 1 minute then gradually add the milk, stirring until evenly blended. Bring the sauce slowly to the boil, stirring constantly until it thickens. Cook over a low heat for 2 minutes.

3 Remove the pan from the heat and leave to cool slightly, then beat in the cheese, egg yolks and herbs and season with salt and pepper. Whisk the egg whites until stiff and fold into the sauce until evenly incorporated.

4 Pour the mixture into the prepared tin and cook in a preheated oven, 200°C (400°F), Gas Mark 6, for 12–15 minutes until risen and firm to the touch. Remove from the oven and set aside to cool. Reduce the oven temperature to 190°C (375°F), Gas Mark 5.

5 While the roulade is cooking, prepare the filling. Beat together the cheese and half the oil until smooth and season with nutmeg and salt and pepper.

6 Heat the remaining oil in a frying pan and fry the leek for 5 minutes. Drain the spinach well, squeeze out all the excess liquid and chop finely. Add to the leeks and cook gently for 5 minutes.

7 To assemble the roulade, turn it out of the tin and carefully peel away the paper. Spread over the softened cheese and then the spinach mixture. Roll up from a short end and place on the oiled Swiss roll tin. Brush with oil and bake for 20–25 minutes. Serve hot, in slices, with the fresh tomato sauce.

herb omelette with **mustard** mushrooms

1 tablespoon wholegrain mustard
50 g/2 oz butter, softened
4 flat mushrooms
2 tablespoons chopped mixed fresh herbs (chives, parsley and tarragon)
4 eggs
salt and pepper

If you prefer, cook half the egg mixture at a time to make two smaller omelettes.

1 Beat the mustard into 40 g/1½ of the butter and spread over the undersides of the mushrooms. Put them on a foil-lined grill pan and cook for 5–6 minutes until golden and tender. Remove and keep warm.

2 Meanwhile, beat the herbs into the eggs and season to taste with salt and pepper.

3 Melt the remaining butter in an omelette pan or nonstick frying pan, swirl in the egg mixture, and cook until almost set. Carefully slide out the omelette and flip it over on to a warmed plate, add the mushrooms and serve.

green **bean** and **chorizo** omelette

150 g/5 oz green beans, cut into short lengths

1 tablespoon olive oil

15 g/½ oz butter

1 red onion, chopped

4 eggs, beaten

25 g/1 oz chorizo sausage, thinly sliced

50 g/2 oz Cheddar cheese, grated

salt and pepper

The spicy, garlicky chorizo sausage adds colour and bite to a simple omelette. Serve with some warm, crusty bread and a simple tomato and olive salad for an easy meal.

1 Put the green beans into a saucepan of lightly salted boiling water and cook for 4 minutes, then drain.

2 Heat the oil and butter in an omelette or nonstick frying pan. Add the onion and fry gently for 3 minutes until softened. Add the eggs and season with salt and pepper. Cook gently for 2–3 minutes until they are lightly set, pushing the cooked edges of the omelette towards the centre so the uncooked mixture fills the pan.

3 Scatter the beans and chorizo over the omelette and then sprinkle it with the Cheddar cheese. Place under a preheated moderate grill for about 2 minutes until the cheese has melted.

spinach and **ricotta** ravioli

Pasta:
400 g/13 oz plain white flour
1 teaspoon salt
1 tablespoon olive oil
4 eggs, beaten

Filling:
750 g/1½ lb fresh spinach, cooked
175 g/6 oz fresh ricotta or curd cheese
½ teaspoon grated nutmeg
1 teaspoon salt
pepper
beaten egg, to seal

To serve:
125 g/4 oz butter, melted
25 g/1 oz Parmesan cheese, freshly grated

1 To make the pasta, sift the flour and salt on to a clean work surface and make a well in the centre with your fist. Pour in the oil and beaten eggs and gradually mix into the flour with the fingers of one hand.

2 Knead the pasta until smooth, then wrap it in clingfilm and leave to rest for at least 30 minutes before attempting to roll it out. The pasta will be much more elastic after resting.

3 To make the filling, put the spinach and ricotta into a food processor with the nutmeg and salt and pepper to taste and process until smooth. Cover and chill while you roll out the dough.

4 Cut the dough in half and wrap one half in clingfilm. Roll out the other half thinly to a rectangle on a lightly floured surface. Cover with a damp tea towel and repeat with the remaining dough.

5 Spoon or pipe small mounds of the filling in even rows on to one sheet of pasta, spacing them at 4 cm/1½ inch intervals. With a pastry brush, brush the spaces of dough between the mounds with beaten egg. Using a rolling pin, lift the remaining sheet of pasta over the sheet with the filling. Press down firmly between the mounds of filling, pushing out any pockets of trapped air.

6 Cut the pasta into squares with a serrated ravioli cutter or sharp knife, or cut it into semi-circles with an upturned glass. Transfer them to a floured tea towel and leave to rest for 1 hour before cooking.

7 Bring a large saucepan of salted water to the boil. Toss in the ravioli and cook in batches for 3 minutes until puffy. Drain well and toss with melted butter. Serve immediately with freshly grated Parmesan.

curried **parsnip** and **cheese** soufflés

250 g/8 oz peeled parsnips, chopped

25 g/1 oz butter, plus extra for greasing

25 g/1 oz plain flour

2 teaspoons hot curry paste

200 ml/7 fl oz milk

40 g/1½ oz Gruyère or Cheddar cheese, grated

3 eggs, separated

2 tablespoons chopped coriander leaves

40 g/1½ oz ground almonds, toasted

salt and pepper

Don't be put off cooking soufflés because of their reputation for collapsing the moment they arrive at the table. As long as the taste is great, it doesn't really matter if they don't look perfect.

1 Steam the parsnips for 15–20 minutes until tender. Mash well and set aside to cool.

2 Melt the butter in a small saucepan, add the flour and cook for 1 minute, stirring. Stir in the curry paste and gradually add the milk, stirring constantly until smooth. Slowly bring to the boil, stirring constantly until thickened. Cook over a low heat for 2 minutes.

3 Remove the pan from the heat and stir in the grated cheese until it has melted. Cool slightly, then beat in the egg yolks with the cooled mashed parsnip, chopped coriander, half the toasted ground almonds and salt and pepper to taste.

4 Whisk the egg whites until stiff and carefully fold into the parsnip mixture until evenly incorporated.

5 Grease 6 large ramekin dishes and line with the remaining toasted ground almonds. Spoon in the soufflé mixture and place the ramekin dishes in a large roasting tin. Add enough boiling water to come two-thirds of the way up the sides of the ramekin dishes and place the roasting tin in a preheated oven, 200°C (400°F), Gas Mark 6, for 25 minutes until risen and golden. Serve the soufflés immediately.

layered **cheese** and **tomato** soufflé

25 g/1 oz butter, plus extra for greasing

1 garlic clove, crushed

1 small onion, chopped

375 g/12 oz tomatoes, skinned and chopped

2 teaspoons dried oregano

6–8 black olives, pitted and chopped

salt and pepper

Soufflé Mixture:

40 g/1½ oz butter

40 g/1½ oz plain flour

300 ml/½ pint single cream or milk

3 large eggs, separated

150 g/5 oz full-fat soft cheese with garlic and herbs, crumbled

A soufflé never fails to impress although it is, in fact, astonishingly easy to make. It is important the soufflé is served immediately it is ready, otherwise it will collapse disappointingly.

1 Melt the butter in a heavy-based saucepan. Add the garlic, onion and tomatoes and fry over a low heat, stirring occasionally, for 3–4 minutes. Add the oregano and olives and season with salt and pepper to taste. Remove the pan from the heat and set aside to cool.

2 Meanwhile, make the soufflé. Melt the butter in a saucepan. Add the flour and cook, stirring, for 1 minute. Remove the pan from the heat and gradually add the cream or milk, stirring vigorously after each addition to ensure that it is fully incorporated. Return the pan to the heat and bring to the boil, stirring until thickened. Remove the pan from the heat and beat in the egg yolks, one at a time. Add the cheese and stir until it has completely melted. Set the pan aside to cool.

3 Whisk the egg whites until just stiff enough to stand in peaks. Mix about 2 tablespoons of the egg whites into the cheese mixture, then carefully fold the remaining egg whites into the cheese mixture with a metal spoon.

4 Grease a 1.5 litre/2½ pint soufflé dish with butter and place it on a baking sheet. Spread the cooled tomato mixture in the dish and cover with the soufflé mixture. Bake immediately in a preheated oven, 190°C (375°F), Gas Mark 5, for 35–40 minutes, until well risen and golden brown. Serve immediately.

eggs baked on **red vegetables**

5 tablespoons olive oil

1 Spanish onion, sliced

4 garlic cloves, crushed

4 red peppers, cored, deseeded and sliced

1 courgette, sliced

5 tomatoes, sliced

2 tablespoons chopped parsley

large pinch of paprika

large pinch of dried chilli flakes

4 eggs

salt and pepper

To garnish:

ground cumin

paprika

4 coriander sprigs

A rich, paprika-red garlicky mixture of slowly cooked red peppers, tomatoes, onion and courgettes makes a bed full of flavour on which to cook eggs. The eggs should only be lightly cooked so that the yolks will flow as a contrasting creamy sauce over the vegetables.

1 Heat the oil in a large frying pan. Add the onion and fry briskly until golden. Add the garlic, red peppers, courgette and tomatoes and simmer for 15–20 minutes, stirring occasionally, until all the vegetables are soft.

2 Stir in the parsley, paprika and chilli flakes and season to taste with salt and pepper. Simmer for a further 5 minutes.

3 Spoon the vegetable mixture into a large shallow ovenproof dish. Make 4 indentations in the vegetable mixture and break an egg into each one. Bake in a preheated oven, 160°C (325°F), Gas Mark 3, for 10 minutes until the egg whites are just set and the yolks are still creamy.

4 To serve, sprinkle ground cumin and paprika over the eggs and garnish with coriander sprigs.

hashed **sweet potatoes** with **eggs**

375 g/12 oz sweet potatoes

3 tablespoons olive or vegetable oil

1 red onion, chopped

1 garlic clove, crushed (optional)

2 teaspoons paprika

1 red pepper, cored, deseeded and chopped

1 green pepper, cored, deseeded and chopped

2 eggs

Sweet potatoes have a distinctive, earthy sweetness that goes well with peppers and onion. For this recipe, you could use half sweet potatoes and half ordinary potatoes or even just ordinary potatoes if you prefer.

1 Scrub the sweet potatoes and cut them into 1 cm/½ inch dice. Put them in a pan of boiling water and cook for 5 minutes until softened. Drain thoroughly.

2 Heat the oil in a heavy-based frying pan. Add the onion and sweet potato and fry gently for about 5 minutes until beginning to colour. Add the garlic, if using, paprika and peppers and fry for a further 5 minutes.

3 Once the vegetables are soft and pale golden, make two indentations in the mixture, each large enough to take an egg. Break an egg into each cavity and cook gently until set. Place the pan under a preheated moderate grill to finish cooking the eggs. Serve immediately.

panzanella

2 eggs

300 g/10 oz tomatoes, cut into wedges

6 pitted black olives

2 sun-dried tomatoes in oil, drained and thinly sliced

1 tablespoon balsamic vinegar

a few torn basil leaves

salt and pepper

Croûtons:

1 small, crusty sesame roll, cut into cubes

2 tablespoons olive oil

Based on the classic Italian salad, this peasant dish is a colourful combination of fresh tomatoes, black olives, hard-boiled eggs and golden croûtons, with a fresh basil and balsamic vinegar dressing. The salad can be made in advance, but don't add the croûtons until the last minute or they will go soggy.

1 Put the eggs into a small saucepan of water, bring to the boil and cook for 10 minutes, until hard boiled.

2 Meanwhile, to make the croûtons, put the cubes of bread into a plastic bag with the oil and toss together. Transfer the bread to a baking sheet and place in a preheated oven, 200°C (400°F), Gas Mark 6, for 8–10 minutes, until crisp and golden.

3 Drain the eggs and crack the shells. Fill the saucepan with cold water, put the eggs back in and leave them to cool.

4 Put the tomatoes, olives and sun-dried tomatoes into a salad bowl. Add the vinegar and basil and salt and pepper to taste, then toss together.

5 Cut the eggs into wedges and add to the salad with the warm croûtons, then spoon on to plates.

salmon fish cakes with spinach and poached eggs

250 g/8 oz King Edward potatoes, quartered

300 g/10 oz salmon fillet, skinned and bones removed

1–2 tablespoons plain flour

6–8 tablespoons sunflower or groundnut oil

500 g/1 lb fresh spinach, washed

1 tablespoon vinegar

4 eggs

sea salt and pepper

lemon wedges, to serve

Salmon fish cakes are some of the finest and are quick to make and cook. If you particularly like raw salmon and have a very fresh piece of salmon fillet, you can make a very fine raw fish cake – a salmon tartare of very finely chopped fillet topped with tiny capers and finely chopped hard-boiled egg and parsley.

1 Put the potatoes into a saucepan of boiling water and boil until they are just cooked when pierced with a sharp knife. Drain well and leave to cool.

2 Either roughly chop the salmon or process it briefly in a food processor to make a coarse mince. Using a fork or the back of a wooden spoon, roughly mash the potatoes with salt and pepper. Add the minced salmon and mix together.

3 With floured hands, divide the mixture into 4 pieces and press firmly into 4 plump fish cakes. Coat each fish cake in flour and chill in the refrigerator for 1 hour.

4 Put the oil in a large frying pan and heat until hot. Add the fish cakes to the hot oil and cook for 3–4 minutes on each side.

5 Put the spinach into a saucepan with just the water that clings to the leaves and cover with a lid. Heat gently for 2–3 minutes or until the spinach has just begun to wilt. Drain the spinach thoroughly and season with a little salt and pepper.

6 Poach the eggs in a pan of gently simmering water for 3–4 minutes until just cooked. Remove the fish cakes from the oil and set them on individual plates, top each one with some of the spinach and finish with a hot poached egg. Serve with lemon wedges.

kedgeree with **artichokes** and **rosemary butter**

6 eggs

250 g/8 oz basmati rice

50 g/2 oz butter, melted

1 tablespoon chopped rosemary

1 tablespoon chopped chives

1 tablespoon lime juice

2 tablespoons olive oil

1 onion, chopped

1 teaspoon coriander seeds, crushed

1 teaspoon fennel seeds, crushed

425 g/14 oz can artichoke hearts, rinsed, drained and halved

salt and pepper

lime wedges, to garnish

Packed with delicious flavours, this is a great vegetarian alternative to a traditional kedgeree.

1 Hard-boil the eggs according to the instructions on page 7, then cool in cold water. Cook the rice in plenty of lightly salted boiling water for about 10 minutes or until just tender.

2 Meanwhile, mix together the melted butter, rosemary, chives and lime juice and season with salt and pepper. Keep warm.

3 Heat the oil in a frying pan. Add the onion, coriander seeds and fennel seeds and fry gently for 5 minutes. Drain the rice and add to the pan with the artichoke hearts, season to taste with salt and pepper and heat through gently for 1 minute. Shell the eggs and cut lengthways into quarters, then lightly stir them in.

4 Transfer the rice to serving plates and pour over the herb butter. Serve garnished with lime wedges.

tuna kedgeree

250 g/8 oz basmati rice

100 g/3 ½ oz frozen baby broad beans

4 eggs

400 g/13 oz can tuna in oil or brine, drained

25 g/1 oz unsalted butter

1 small onion, finely chopped

1 teaspoon medium curry paste

small handful of flat leaf parsley, chopped

salt and pepper

flat leaf parsley sprigs, to garnish

lemon or lime wedges, to serve

1 Cook the rice in plenty of lightly salted boiling water for about 8 minutes until almost tender. Add the broad beans and cook for a further 3 minutes; drain.

2 Meanwhile, hard-boil the eggs according to the instructions on page 7, then cool in cold water. Flake the tuna into small chunks, then shell the eggs and cut lengthways into quarters.

3 Melt the butter in a large frying pan, add the onion and curry paste and fry gently for 3 minutes. Add the drained rice, broad beans, tuna and eggs.

4 Stir in the parsley and season the kedgeree with salt and pepper to taste. Stir gently over a low heat for 1 minute, then transfer to serving plates. Garnish with parsley and serve with lemon or lime wedges.

griddled bacon-wrapped **scallops**

12 smoked streaky bacon rashers
12 large scallops, cleaned
4 eggs or quails' eggs
200 g/7 oz mixed salad leaves
4 tablespoons olive oil
4 tablespoons lemon juice
sea salt and pepper

To garnish:
grated lemon rind
snipped chives

Take care not to overcook the scallops or they will become tough.

1 Heat a griddle pan. Wrap a rasher of bacon around each scallop and secure with a cocktail stick. Place on the griddle and cook for 8 minutes, turning the scallops to give the bacon an even colour.

2 Meanwhile, soft-boil the eggs according to the instructions on page 00. Shell the eggs carefully. Toss the mixed leaf salad in a large serving dish with the olive oil and lemon juice and season with salt and pepper to taste.

3 When the scallops are cooked, arrange them on top of the salad. Finally, break the soft-boiled eggs in half, add to the salad and serve quickly before all the yolk runs out. Garnish with lemon rind and snipped chives.

banana curry

4 eggs

50 g/2 oz butter

2 small onions, chopped

75 g/3 oz sultanas

1 dessert apple, peeled, cored and diced

½ teaspoon salt

40 g/1½ oz flour

2 teaspoons curry powder

300 ml/½ pint coconut milk

300 ml/½ pint water

4 under-ripe green bananas, peeled and sliced diagonally

To serve:

mango chutney

boiled rice

1 Hard-boil the eggs according to the instructions on page 7, then cool in cold water. Shell the eggs and cut lengthways into quarters.

2 Melt the butter in a large heavy-based saucepan. Add the onions and fry gently over very low heat until they are softened and translucent. Take care that they do not brown.

3 Meanwhile, soak the sultanas in a little boiling water for 2–3 minutes to plump them up. Drain and add to the onions with the apple and salt. Stir in the flour and curry powder and cook, stirring constantly, for 3–4 minutes.

4 Remove the saucepan from the heat and gradually stir in the coconut milk and water, a little at a time. Return the pan to the heat and cook very gently, stirring until thickened.

5 Add the bananas and continue cooking gently over low heat for about 7 minutes. Add the eggs to the curry and heat through. Serve with mango chutney and plain boiled rice.

4 Desserts

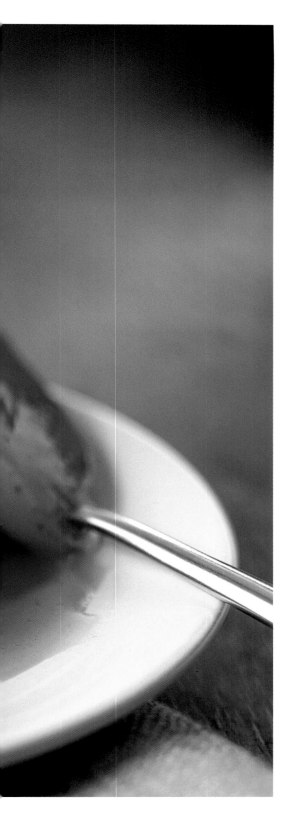

chocolate and **banana** pancake torte

50 g/2 oz ground hazelnuts or almonds, toasted

1 teaspoon almond extract

4 tablespoons milk

1 quantity Sweet Pancake batter (see page 13)

oil or butter, for frying

300 g/10 oz chocolate and hazelnut spread

4 tablespoons double cream

5 large bananas

2 tablespoons lemon juice

icing sugar, for sprinkling

25 g/1 oz hazelnuts, toasted and roughly chopped

single cream, to serve

Although delicious served at room temperature, this dessert can also be heated through before serving. Assemble it on a baking sheet instead of a plate and warm through in a preheated oven, 200°C (400°F), Gas Mark 6, for 10 minutes.

1 Beat the toasted nuts, almond extract and milk into the pancake batter and cook the pancakes following the instructions on page 13. Set the pancakes aside while making the filling.

2 Put the chocolate spread in a small pan with the cream and heat gently until slightly softened but not liquid. Slice the bananas as thinly as possible and toss in the lemon juice.

3 Place a pancake on a flat plate and spread with a little of the chocolate spread. Cover with a thin layer of banana slices. Arrange another pancake on top. Continue layering the ingredients, finishing with a pancake. Sprinkle with icing sugar and scatter with toasted hazelnuts. Serve cut into wedges, with cream.

iced **chocolate** mousse

300 g/10 oz plain dark chocolate,
broken into pieces

3 tablespoons golden syrup

2 tablespoons brandy, orange-
flavoured liqueur or water

5 tablespoons water

100 g/3½ oz cocoa powder

300 ml/½ pint whipping cream

4 egg whites

2 tablespoons caster sugar

pouring cream, to serve

Lightened with whipped cream and egg whites, this rich iced dessert has a mousse-like texture. Here it's frozen in little pudding moulds, then turned out for serving, but you can freeze it in ramekin dishes or even in a tub to serve it in scoops like ice cream.

1 Melt the chocolate with the golden syrup and the brandy, liqueur or water, plus the 5 tablespoons water. Stir until smooth, then stir in the cocoa powder. Pour into a large bowl and leave until cold.

2 Whip the cream until just peaking. Whisk the egg whites in a separate bowl until stiff, then gradually whisk in the sugar.

3 Using a large metal spoon, fold the whipped cream and then the egg whites into the chocolate mixture until evenly combined. Spoon into 6 individual metal pudding moulds or dariole moulds and freeze for at least 4 hours.

4 To serve, dip the moulds very briefly in hot water. Run a small knife around the edge of each mousse to check that it has loosened from the mould. Tap out on to serving plates. Serve with pouring cream.

chocolate marble cheesecake

125 g/4 oz gingersnap biscuits
2 tablespoons cocoa powder
40 g/1½ oz unsalted butter

Filling:
400 g/13 oz cream cheese
150 g/5 oz caster sugar
3 eggs
2 teaspoons vanilla extract
150 ml/¼ pint double cream
200 g/7 oz plain dark chocolate, broken into pieces
pouring cream, to serve

When baked, the centre of this cheesecake should still feel slightly soft in the middle. Avoid overbaking or the texture will be dry.

1 Put the biscuits into a polythene bag and crush them with a rolling pin. Mix the crushed biscuits with the cocoa powder. Melt the butter in a small saucepan and stir in the biscuit mixture until combined. Press the mixture into the base of a 20 cm/8 inch springform cake tin.

2 Beat the cream cheese to soften, then beat in the sugar, eggs, vanilla extract and cream. Melt the chocolate. Spoon about one-third of the cream cheese mixture into a separate bowl and beat in the chocolate.

3 Pour the cream cheese mixture into the tin, then place spoonfuls of the cream cheese and chocolate mixture over it. Using a knife, swirl the mixtures together lightly to create a marbled effect.

4 Bake in a preheated oven, 160°C (325°F), Gas Mark 3, for 35–40 minutes or until the centre of the cheesecake feels only just set. Turn off the oven and leave the cheesecake to cool in it, then transfer to the refrigerator. Serve chilled with pouring cream.

hot
chocolate custard

1 tablespoon plain flour
2 tablespoons cocoa powder
200 g/7 oz sugar
2 egg yolks, beaten
450 ml/¾ pint milk
1 tablespoon brandy
1 tablespoon chopped walnuts
15 g/½ oz butter
chopped walnuts, to decorate
vanilla ice cream, to serve

1 Thoroughly mix the flour, cocoa and sugar in a bowl. Add the egg yolks and gradually whisk in the milk until smooth.

2 Pour the mixture into a heavy-based saucepan and cook, whisking continuously, until the custard boils. Reduce the heat to low and cook for 4–5 minutes, still whisking continuously.

3 Remove the pan from the heat and beat in the brandy, walnuts and butter until well mixed. Pour the custard into serving dishes and decorate with chopped walnuts. Serve at once, with scoops of vanilla ice cream.

warm **espresso chocolate** pots

175 g/6 oz plain dark chocolate, chopped

250 ml/8 fl oz strong espresso coffee

2 tablespoons whisky

50 g/2 oz sugar

6 egg yolks

50 ml/2 fl oz double cream

grated nutmeg

Use a good quality dark chocolate with a high percentage of cocoa butter – at least 75%.

1 Place the chocolate in a small saucepan with the coffee and whisky and heat gently until the chocolate has melted. Add the sugar and stir until dissolved. Remove from the heat.

2 Immediately beat in the egg yolks until the mixture thickens. Pour through a fine sieve into 8 small espresso cups or ramekins. Allow to cool then chill for 4 hours or overnight until set.

3 Whip the cream until it just holds its shape and spoon a little on to each chocolate pot. Sprinkle with nutmeg. Pour a small amount of boiling water into a roasting dish to a depth of about 1 cm/½ inch. Sit the chocolate pots in the boiling water for 1 minute, then remove and serve immediately.

hot **berry** soufflés

15 g/½ oz butter
100 g/3½ oz caster sugar
50 g/2 oz blackberries
200 g/7 oz raspberries
4 large egg whites
icing sugar, to dust
custard or ice cream, to serve
(optional)

These simple soufflés should be made at the last minute, but the fruit can be puréed in advance. Serve them with ice cream – the contrast between hot and cold is very refreshing.

1 Use the butter to grease 4 200 ml/7 fl oz ramekins and then coat the insides evenly with a little of the caster sugar, tipping out the excess sugar. Place the ramekins on a baking sheet.

2 Purée the blackberries and raspberries in a food processor or blender, reserving a few of the berries for decoration, then pour the purée into a bowl. Alternatively, the fruit can be rubbed through a fine sieve to make a smooth purée.

3 Place the egg whites in a large, perfectly clean bowl, then use an electric beater to whisk them until they are stiff, but not dry. Gradually sprinkle in the remaining caster sugar, whisking continuously, and carry on whisking until the whites are stiff and shiny.

4 Gently fold the egg whites into the berry purée, then spoon this mixture into the prepared ramekins. Bake immediately in a preheated oven, 190°C (375°F), Gas Mark 5, for 15 minutes or until risen and golden.

5 Dust the soufflés with icing sugar and decorate with the reserved berries. Serve immediately with custard or ice cream if you like.

amaretto almond soufflés

4 macaroons

4 tablespoons Amaretto di Saronno

150 ml/¼ pint milk

1 drop of vanilla extract

15 g/½ oz butter, plus extra for greasing

25 g/1 oz plain flour, plus a little extra for flouring the dishes

4 egg yolks (1 kept separately)

4 egg whites

2 tablespoons granulated sugar

sifted icing sugar, to decorate

Almond Purée:

75 g/3 oz slivered almonds

150 ml/¼ pint milk

2 teaspoons sugar

Doubly delicious for almond fanciers, this fluffy soufflé contains both a purée of almonds and a generous dash of the almond liqueur, Amaretto di Saronno.

1 First make the almond purée. Put the almonds, milk and sugar into a saucepan and bring to the boil. Reduce the heat and simmer gently for a few minutes. Cool slightly and then work in a food processor or blender until thoroughly mixed.

2 Grease and flour 4 7.5 cm/3 inch soufflé dishes. Soak the macaroons in half of the Amaretto and put one macaroon, cut into quarters, into each prepared soufflé dish.

3 To make the soufflés, put two-thirds of the milk into a heavy-based saucepan with the vanilla and butter and bring to the boil. Remove from the heat and stir in the remaining milk with the flour and 1 egg yolk. Heat again until the mixture thickens and whisk briefly. Add the remaining egg yolks and cook for 2 minutes over low heat.

4 Whisk the egg whites until stiff and then whisk in the sugar. Blend the soufflé mixture with the almond purée and the remaining Amaretto. Carefully fold in the beaten egg white. Spoon the mixture into the soufflé dishes and bake in a preheated oven, 220°C (425°F), Gas Mark 7, for 10–12 minutes. Dust with icing sugar and serve immediately.

pear and **cardamom** flan

Shortcrust Pastry:
175 g/6 oz plain flour
pinch of salt
100 g/3½ oz unsalted butter, diced
2 tablespoons caster sugar
1 egg yolk
1–2 tablespoons cold water

Filling:
125 g/4 oz unsalted butter, softened
75 g/3 oz caster sugar
2 small eggs, lightly beaten
75 g/3 oz ground hazelnuts
25 g/1 oz ground rice
seeds from 2 cardamom pods, crushed
1 teaspoon grated lemon rind
4 tablespoons soured cream
3 small firm pears

To serve:
1 teaspoon caster sugar, to serve (optional)
whipped cream

1 To make the pastry, sift the flour and salt into a bowl and rub in the butter until the mixture resembles fine breadcrumbs. Stir in the sugar and gradually work in the egg yolk and water to form a soft dough. Knead lightly, wrap in clingfilm and chill for 30 minutes.

2 Roll out the pastry on a lightly floured surface and use to line a 23 cm/9 inch fluted flan tin. Prick the base with a fork and chill for 20 minutes.

3 Line the pastry case with nonstick baking paper and baking beans and place in a preheated oven, 220°C (425°F), Gas Mark 7, for 10 minutes. Remove the paper and beans and bake for a further 10–12 minutes until the pastry is crisp and golden. Reduce the oven temperature to 180°C (350°F), Gas Mark 4.

4 To make the filling, beat together the butter and sugar in a bowl until pale and light and then gradually beat in the eggs, a little at a time until incorporated. Lightly beat in all the remaining ingredients, except the pears. Pour the mixture into the prepared pastry case.

5 Peel and halve the pears and scoop out the cores. Thinly slice each pear lengthways. Be careful not to change the shape of the pears. Then, using a palette knife, carefully transfer the sliced pears to the pastry case, arranging them neatly on the filling. Bake the flan for 55–60 minutes until golden and firm in the middle. Serve the flan warm, sprinkled with a little caster sugar and some whipped cream, if liked.

plum and **lemon** tart

Shortcrust Pastry:
175 g/6 oz plain flour
75 g/3 oz chilled butter, diced
50 g/2 oz caster sugar
1 egg, beaten

Filling:
50 g/2 oz butter, at room temperature
50 g/2 oz caster sugar
50 g/2 oz semolina
grated rind of 1 lemon
1 egg, beaten
750 g/1½ lb ripe plums, halved and stoned
4 tablespoons apricot jam
whipped cream, to serve

1 To make the pastry, place the flour in a bowl, add the diced butter and rub in with the fingertips until the mixture resembles fine breadcrumbs. Stir in the caster sugar and beaten egg and mix to a firm dough, adding a little water if necessary.

2 Knead the dough briefly on a lightly floured surface, then wrap in clingfilm and chill for 30 minutes. Roll out the pastry and use to line a 23 cm/9 inch flan tin. Prick the pastry base with a fork.

3 To make the filling, beat together the butter and sugar in a bowl until light and fluffy. Beat in the semolina, lemon rind and beaten egg, and then spread the mixture over the pastry base. Arrange the plum halves over the top, cut sides down.

4 Bake the tart in a preheated oven, 190°C (375°F), Gas Mark 5, for 40–45 minutes, until the pastry is browned and the filling golden and set. Warm the jam in a small saucepan, then press it through a sieve into a bowl. Brush the apricot glaze over the top of the tart. Serve warm or cold, with lightly whipped cream.

crème **caramel**

500 ml/17 fl oz milk
1 vanilla pod, split in half
lengthways
4 eggs
50 g/2 oz sugar

Caramel:
50 g/2 oz sugar
1 tablespoon water
1 teaspoon lemon juice

The simple baked egg custard, a universal favourite, becomes a memorably sophisticated dessert in this classic treatment.

1 Put the milk and vanilla pod into a heavy saucepan and bring to the boil. Remove from the heat and leave for 5 minutes to infuse. Place the eggs and sugar in a bowl and whisk until thoroughly combined. Discard the vanilla pod and whisk the milk into the egg and sugar mixture.

2 While the milk is infusing, make the caramel. Put the sugar, water and lemon juice into a small saucepan and cook over a moderate heat, stirring well until the sugar dissolves. When it turns a rich golden caramel colour, remove the pan from the heat immediately.

3 Pour the caramel into 4 small moulds or a 1 litre/1¾ pint charlotte mould. Rotate the moulds quickly so that the caramel coats the base and sides evenly.

4 Strain the custard through a fine sieve. Pour into the moulds and stand them in a bain marie or roasting tin half-filled with water. Cook in a preheated oven, 150°C (300°F), Gas Mark 2, for about 45 minutes or until set. Leave to cool and then chill in the refrigerator before unmoulding. To unmould, dip the base of the moulds into a bowl of hot water for 30 seconds and then turn them out on to a serving plate.

lavender
crème brûlée

600 ml/1 pint single cream
4–6 fresh lavender flower heads, depending on size
6 egg yolks
75 g/3 oz caster sugar
6 teaspoons demerara sugar
fresh lavender, to decorate

Lavender is rarely used in cooking nowadays but it adds a delicate perfume and makes a great talking point in this creamy dessert. Serve the crème brûlées within 2–3 hours of adding the caramel topping otherwise they will begin to soften and lose their wonderful crunchy texture.

1 Pour the cream into a small saucepan, add the lavender heads and gently heat for 2–3 minutes, but do not boil. Remove the pan from the heat and leave to infuse for 30 minutes.

2 Beat together the egg yolks and sugar until smooth. Take the lavender out of the cream with a draining spoon and then reheat the cream, bringing it almost up to the boil. Gradually stir the hot cream into the egg yolk mixture and then strain into a jug or back into the saucepan. Pour into 6 individual ovenproof ramekins or shallow dishes, cover the tops with foil and stand them in a roasting tin. Pour in enough cold water to come halfway up the sides of the dishes and then bake in a preheated oven, 160°C (325°F), Gas Mark 3, for 25–30 minutes until just set.

3 Take the dishes out of the roasting tin and leave to cool at room temperature, then chill for at least 4 hours or overnight in the refrigerator. Sprinkle demerara sugar over the tops of the dishes and cook under a preheated grill or using a blowtorch for 3–5 minutes until the sugar has caramelized. Cool then chill and decorate with sprigs of fresh lavender.

zabaglione

4 egg yolks

75 g/3 oz sugar, plus extra for frosting the glasses

grated rind of ½ lemon

½ teaspoon ground cinnamon, plus extra to decorate

1 drop vanilla extract

125 ml/4 fl oz Marsala

125 g/4 oz fruit (such as peaches, apricots, berries), sliced

1 Put the egg yolks, sugar, lemon rind, cinnamon and vanilla extract into a heatproof bowl and beat with an electric mixer until thick, pale and creamy.

2 Place the bowl over a saucepan of simmering water and continue beating. Slowly add the Marsala and beat until the mixture is warm, frothy and thick.

3 To serve, dip the rims of 4 glasses in water, then in sugar to frost them. Divide the fruit among the glasses, then spoon in the zabaglione. To serve, dust with a little extra cinnamon. Serve immediately

baked **lemon** and **bay** custards

12 bay leaves, bruised
2 tablespoons lemon rind
150 ml/¼ pint double cream
4 eggs
1 egg yolk
150 g/5 oz caster sugar
100 ml/3½ fl oz lemon juice

This recipe is a variation of the old classic lemon tart. Here, the lemon custard is infused with bay leaves, giving it a heady scent. The custard is baked in a very low oven: if the oven is too hot the custard will curdle. Check after 40 minutes – the centres should be almost set but still move a little, they will firm up as they cool.

1 Put the bay leaves, lemon rind and cream in a small saucepan and heat gently until it reaches boiling point. Remove from the heat and set aside for 2 hours to infuse.

2 Whisk together the eggs, egg yolk and sugar until the mixture is pale and creamy and then whisk in the lemon juice. Strain the cream mixture through a fine sieve into the egg mixture and stir until combined.

3 Pour the custard into 4 individual ramekins and place on a baking sheet. Bake in a preheated oven, 120°C (250°F), Gas Mark ½, for 50 minutes or until the custards are almost set in the middle. Leave until cold and chill until required. Return to room temperature before serving.

bread and **butter** pudding

40 g/1½ oz butter
4 slices white bread, crusts removed
4 tablespoons apricot jam
25 g/1 oz cut mixed peel
25 g/1 oz sultanas
450 ml/¾ pint milk
2 tablespoons sugar
2 eggs, beaten

If you like, add a tablespoon of sherry when you whisk in the eggs.

1 Grease a 1.2 litre/2 pint ovenproof serving dish with 15 g/½ oz of the butter.

2 Butter the bread and spread with the apricot jam. Cut the slices into small triangles. Layer the bread triangles in the dish, sprinkling the mixed peel and sultanas between the layers.

3 Put the milk and sugar into a saucepan and heat to just below boiling point. Remove from the heat and whisk in the eggs. Strain the mixture over the bread and leave to soak for 30 minutes.

4 Place the dish in a roasting tin and fill with water to halfway up the sides and bake in a preheated oven, 180°C (350°F), Gas Mark 4, for 45 minutes. Increase the heat to 190°C (375°F), Gas Mark 5 and cook for a further 10–15 minutes until crisp and golden on top and just set. Serve at once.

exotic **fruit** clafoutis

500 g/1 lb fresh pineapple and mango, peeled

2 tablespoons dark rum

3 eggs

20 g/¾ oz plain flour

pinch of salt

50 g/2 oz caster sugar

300 ml/½ pint milk

1 vanilla pod

butter, for greasing

caster sugar, for sprinkling

This exotic fruit batter pudding comes from the French Caribbean island of Guadeloupe.

1 Cut the fresh pineapple and the mango flesh into 1 cm/½ inch chunks. Put the prepared fruit in a bowl and sprinkle with the rum. Set aside.

2 To make the batter, break the eggs into a bowl and beat lightly together. Sift in the flour and salt and blend well with the beaten eggs. Whisk in the sugar until the mixture is smooth.

3 Heat the milk with the vanilla pod but do not allow to boil. Remove from the heat and leave to infuse for 5 minutes. Remove the vanilla pod and strain the milk into the egg mixture, a little at a time, beating well until thoroughly blended. Beat in the rum from the soaked fruit.

4 Arrange the pineapple and mango in a buttered shallow, ovenproof dish. Pour the batter mixture over them and bake in a preheated oven, 200°C (400°F), Gas Mark 6, for 25–30 minutes, until risen and set. Cool a little and serve lukewarm, sprinkled with caster sugar.

sweet **cheese** with soft **fruits**

50 g/2 oz caster sugar

3 tablespoons water

2–3 fresh lavender flowers (optional)

1 egg white

500 g/1 lb Quark

175 g/6 oz crème fraîche

mint sprigs, to decorate

Fruit Syrup:

25 g/1 oz caster sugar

2 tablespoons water

250 g/8 oz mixed soft fruit, such as raspberries, blueberries and blackberries

Soft and creamy, this dessert is the perfect partner with soft berry fruits. Ideally, make them in the traditional china heart-shaped perforated coeur de la crème moulds. If they are not available, use small teacups or ramekins, but remember that the desserts may be a little wetter since the excess water has not had been able to drain away.

1 Put the caster sugar and water in a small saucepan and simmer gently until the sugar has dissolved. Add the lavender flowers to the syrup, if using, and simmer for 3 minutes. Remove from the heat and leave to cool.

2 Whisk the egg white in a clean bowl until standing in stiff peaks. Place the Quark and crème fraîche in a bowl. Stir in the cold lavender syrup, then fold in the whisked egg white.

3 Line 4 moulds with damp pieces of muslin and stand them on a plate to catch the liquid that will drip out of the bottom of the moulds. Spoon the cheese mixture into the muslin-lined moulds, level the surface and chill overnight.

4 .To make the fruit syrup, put the caster sugar and water in a small saucepan and heat gently to dissolve the sugar. Add half the fruit to the warm syrup and cook for 1 minute, then remove from the heat. When the syrup and fruit are cold stir in the remaining fruit.

5 Turn the cheeses out of their moulds. Serve with the soft fruits and decorated with mint sprigs.

pavlova

4 egg whites
250 g/8 oz caster sugar
1 tablespoon cornflour
2 teaspoons vinegar
¼ teaspoon vanilla extract

Filling:
300 ml/½ pint double cream
2 bananas, sliced
1 small pineapple, cut into cubes
flesh and juice of 2 passion fruit
2 peaches, skinned and sliced

Vary the filling of the pavlova as you like. Raspberries, strawberries, grapes, figs and redcurrants are all delicious.

1 Whisk the egg whites until stiff. Add the sugar, a tablespoon at a time, whisking until the meringue is very stiff. Whisk in the cornflour, vinegar and vanilla.

2 Pile the meringue on to a baking sheet lined with nonstick baking paper and spread into a 23 cm/9 inch round. Hollow out the centre slightly and bake in a preheated oven, 150°C (300°F), Gas Mark 2, for 1½ hours.

3 Let the pavlova cool, then remove the paper and place the pavlova on a serving dish. Whip the cream until stiff and fold in some of the fruit. Pile into the pavlova and decorate with the remaining fruit.

lime meringue pie

Shortcrust Pastry:
175 g/6 oz plain flour
100 g/3½ oz chilled butter, diced
25 g caster sugar
1 egg yolk
2–3 tablespoons cold water

Filling:
grated rind and juice of 3 limes
175 g/6 oz caster sugar
3 eggs, beaten
250 g/8 oz butter

Meringue:
3 egg whites
75 g/3 oz caster sugar

1 To make the pastry, place the flour in a bowl, add the diced butter and rub in with the fingertips until the mixture resembles fine breadcrumbs. Stir in the caster sugar and gradually work in the egg yolk and water to make a firm dough.

2 Knead the dough briefly on a lightly floured surface, then wrap in clingfilm and chill for 30 minutes. Roll out the pastry and use to line a 23 cm/9 inch flan tin. Prick the pastry base with a fork and chill for 20 minutes.

3 Line the pastry case with nonstick baking paper and baking beans and place in a preheated oven, 220°C (425°F), Gas Mark 7, for 10 minutes. Remove the paper and beans and bake for a further 10–12 minutes until the pastry is crisp and golden. Remove from the oven and reduce the temperature to 190°C (375°F), Gas Mark 5.

4 To make the pie filling, put the grated lime rind and juice in a heavy-based saucepan with the caster sugar and eggs. Place over a very low heat and stir well.

5 Cut the butter into small dice and add to the lime mixture in the pan, one cube at a time. Continue stirring all the time over a low heat, until all the butter has been incorporated and the mixture is hot.

6 Pour the lime mixture into the prepared pastry case and return to the oven for about 10 minutes, or until the filling is just set. Remove from the oven and allow to cool. Keep the oven at the same temperature while you make the meringue topping.

7 Beat the egg whites until they stand in stiff peaks. Gradually beat in the caster sugar, a little at a time. Pile the meringue on top of the lime filling and bake in the oven for 12–15 minutes, until the meringue is delicately browned. Serve hot or cold.

raspberry and **peach** mallow

2 ripe peaches, stoned and roughly chopped

1 tablespoon water

40 g/1½ oz caster sugar, plus 1 tablespoon

250 g/8 oz raspberries

2 egg whites

½ teaspoon vanilla extract

Greek yogurt, to serve (optional)

Warming summer fruits in a light syrup really brings out their flavours. Here raspberries and peaches are enhanced in this way, then topped with a soft airy meringue, to make an easy, fast pudding for the whole family. Serve warm.

1 Put the peaches into a small saucepan with the water and the 1 tablespoon of sugar. Heat very gently until the peaches are slightly softened and juicy. Stir in the raspberries and then divide the fruits among 4 large ramekins or small heatproof bowls.

2 Whisk the egg whites in a clean bowl until stiffly peaking, using a hand-held electric whisk. Gradually whisk in the sugar, a little at a time, until the mixture is glossy. Whisk in the vanilla extract.

3 Spoon the meringue over the fruits, spreading it to the edges of the dishes and piling it up in the centre. Lightly peak the meringue with the back of a spoon. Bake in a preheated oven, 220°C (425°F), Gas Mark 7, for about 5 minutes until the meringue is golden, keeping a close eye on the meringue as it will colour very quickly. Serve warm with Greek yogurt, if liked.

raspberry meringue nests

3 chocolate flakes

4 egg whites

200 g/7 oz caster sugar

1 teaspoon cornflour

1 teaspoon white wine vinegar

150 ml/¼ pint double cream

325 g/11 oz raspberries

Chocolate Sauce:

200 g/7 oz plain chocolate, broken into pieces

4 tablespoons milk

3 tablespoons golden syrup

½ teaspoon vanilla extract

25 g/1 oz unsalted butter

These individual pavlovas should be crisp on the outside and marshmallowy inside. The chocolate sauce, which may be served either warm or cold, can be spooned over just before serving.

1 Line a large baking sheet with nonstick baking paper. Coarsely crumble the chocolate flakes into a bowl.

2 Whisk the egg whites in a large bowl until stiff. Gradually whisk in the sugar, 1 tablespoon at a time, until the meringue is stiff and glossy. Stir in the cornflour, vinegar and two-thirds of the crumbled chocolate flakes. Divide the mixture into 8 mounds on the prepared baking sheet, spreading each one to about 7 cm/3 inches in diameter and making a dip in the centre. Bake in a preheated oven, 140°C (275°F), Gas Mark 1, for 45–50 minutes, until crisp. Set aside to cool.

3 To make the sauce, put the chocolate, milk, golden syrup and vanilla extract into a small heavy-based saucepan and heat gently, stirring frequently, until the chocolate has melted. Stir in the butter. Continue stirring until the sauce is smooth, then pour it into a jug.

4 Whip the cream, fold in the raspberries and spoon the mixture on to the meringues. Decorate with the remaining crumbled chocolate flakes and serve with the chocolate sauce.

apricot and orange sorbet

150 g/5 oz caster sugar

300 ml/½ pint water

75 ml/3 fl oz fresh orange juice

3 tablespoons fresh lemon juice

grated rind of 1 orange

500 g/1 lb ripe apricots, halved and stoned

1 egg white

sugared mint strips, for decoration (optional)

1 Put the sugar, water, orange and lemon juices and orange rind into a saucepan and bring to the boil, stirring until the sugar has dissolved. Increase the heat and boil rapidly for about 5 minutes until the syrup registers 110°C (225°F) on a sugar thermometer. Add the apricots and simmer gently for about 2 minutes, until they have softened slightly. Leave them to cool in the syrup.

2 Pour the fruit and syrup into a food processor or blender and process to a smooth purée.* Pour into a freezer container, cover and freeze for about 2 hours until frozen around the sides but slushy in the centre.

3 Tip the frozen syrup into a bowl and whisk briefly until smooth. Whisk the egg white briefly until it forms soft peaks and fold into the fruit using a metal spoon. Pour the mixture back into the container and freeze for about 6 hours.

4 Transfer the sorbet to the refrigerator about 20 minutes before serving to soften slightly. To serve, arrange scoops of sorbet in individual glasses and decorate with sugared mint strips, if liked.

★ If using an ice cream machine follow the recipe until halfway through step 2, then pour the mixture into the machine and freeze until half-frozen. Whisk the egg whites until they form soft peaks and add to the half-frozen mixture. Continue to freeze until completely frozen. Follow the serving suggestion at the end of step 4.

honeyed banana
ice cream with **nuts**

500 g/1 lb bananas, peeled
2 tablespoons lemon juice
3 tablespoons thick honey
150 ml/¼ pint natural yogurt
50 g/2 oz chopped nuts
150 ml/¼ pint double or whipping cream
2 egg whites
pralines, for serving (optional)

1 Put the bananas into a bowl with the lemon juice and mash until smooth. Stir in the honey, then the yogurt and nuts and beat well.

2 Whip the cream until it forms soft peaks and fold into the banana mixture.* Transfer the mixture to a freezer container, cover and freeze until partially set.

3 Whisk the egg whites until stiff. Beat the banana mixture to break up the ice crystals, then fold in the egg whites and freeze until firm. Serve with pralines if you like.

★ If using an ice cream machine follow the recipe until halfway through step 2. Transfer the banana mixture to the ice cream machine and churn and freeze until half frozen. Whisk the egg whites until they form soft peaks, then add to the half-frozen mixture. Continue to freeze until completely frozen. Follow the serving suggestion at the end of step 3.

index

ACKNOWLEDGEMENTS

Executive Editor: Sarah Ford
Editor: Rachel Lawrence
Executive Art Editor: Joanna Bennett
Designer: Claire Harvey
Production Controller: Lucy Woodhead
Picture Researcher: Jennifer Veall

Special Photography: Steven Conroy
Food Stylist: David Morgan

All other photography: Octopus Publishing Group Limited/Frank Adam 8/Gus Filgate 35 bottom centre, 39, 40,41, 97/Jeremy Hopley 17 bottom centre, 68-69, 89/David Jordan 69 top right, 79, 91,120/Sandra Lane 24, 57/William Lingwood 33, 69 bottom right/David Loftus 85/Neil Mersh 100, 103/Sean Myers 19, William Reavell 37, 61, 62, 95 bottom centre/Simon Smith 6, 7, 9, 10, 11, 12, 13, 14, 15, 83, 121/Ian Wallace 17 top right, 17 bottom right, 23, 27, 29, 35 top right, 43, 45, 46, 47, 52, 65, 66, 73, 75, 81, 95 top right, 95 bottom right, 99, 116